Guard Rails

Build Your Business and Self Through
Insights and Innovative Thinking

Karl R. LaPan

AuthorHouse™
1663 Liberty Drive
Bloomington, IN 47403
www.authorhouse.com
Phone: 1 (800) 839-8640

Published by AuthorHouse 08/01/2018

ISBN: 978-1-5462-5302-0 (sc)
ISBN: 978-1-5462-5301-3 (e)

Library of Congress Control Number: 2018908800

Print information available on the last page.

Any people depicted in stock imagery provided by Getty Images are models,
and such images are being used for illustrative purposes only.
Certain stock imagery © Getty Images.

This book is printed on acid-free paper.

Guard Rails

Guard Rails: Build Your Business and Self Through Insights and Innovative Thinking

Karl R. LaPan

Contents

Foreword

Guard Rails are loosely defined as a "system designed to keep people (or vehicles) from straying into dangerous or off-limit areas."[1] This is the exact intent of this book. This book highlights practical advice to expand your thinking and provides guardrails to ensure context and structure for applying this book to your business and personal life.

The insights and innovation included are meant to push your thinking and perspective toward new approaches for issues entrepreneurs and business builders face.

Where do you find your inspiration? From ideas, people, or travel? From attending conferences, interacting with people who think differently than you, reading books, talking to strangers, hanging out in a bookstore or brewery, or thinking in the shower? Ideas, insights, inspirations, and innovations are everywhere. The secret sauce is how you connect them, and what insights you draw from them.

Over the past eighteen years, and through my continued role at The NIIC (Northeast Indiana Innovation Center), it's been my privilege and honor to work with thousands of business

---

[1] http://craigsroda.com/guardrails-life/

builders, innovators, big thinkers, and entrepreneurs. They energize, inspire, and motivate me. They drive me to be better, think bigger, and often challenge my perspectives.

I have seen firsthand how innovation and entrepreneurship have benefited communities around the globe. Today, information is rampant and rapid; you perhaps feel there's barely enough time to consume it and connect the dots. Leaders and companies that consume information and act on it are rewarded. Those that don't are likely to be cannibalized and forced into relic status.

Speaking of perspectives, this book is derived from a collection of blogs I've written over the past two years. Topics include innovation, leadership, starting, growing, and scaling a business. It can be challenging to find the time to consume a full-length book consistently, so this book is designed to be digestible and accessible for people in all stages of a business pursuit (as well those who support entrepreneurs). These thoughts are enduring and timeless. I hope you or someone you know will benefit from the fusion of innovation and insights into *actions*.

Through the different topical areas, it is my hope that you will gain some of the interdisciplinary skills to see around corners, to sidestep potholes, and to overcome barriers standing in the way of greater success and significance. Through leaning into your problems and opportunities, you can emerge a smarter and more adept leader.

I am proud to lead The NIIC, where every day we help business builders launch and organizations grow. It surely does take a community—an entrepreneurial community like The NIIC in collaboration with so many others—to help make big dreams come true.

The NIIC serves businesses at every stage, from aspiring entrepreneurs, startups and growing businesses, to high-performance companies and business builders and visionaries in progressive nonprofit organizations ready to scale. Our goal is to give your venture a competitive edge, and help it thrive.

Aspire Higher!

Karl R. LaPan
President and CEO, The NIIC

Proceeds from this book will benefit our Connected Communities Initiative which is focused on inclusive business builders – women, students, people of color, immigrants, and the hardest to employ. The NIIC aspires to be a top entrepreneurial destination of choice and works to accomplish this through a consistent commitment to excellence, adaptive learning, and real-time feedback.

Topical Content Areas

Failure Savvy

It's no secret that our worst fear is often failure. But what if failure were actually a good thing? How do we avoid allowing the fear to cripple people and organizations? Learn about the causes, attitudes, circumstances, and lessons surrounding failure.

Leadership and Culture

One buzzword we encounter almost every day is *culture*. What do we really mean by this? What factors contribute to a positive culture? How can leaders infuse a culture into their organization's DNA? In this section, we examine the intersection of leadership and culture—and what it means for high-potential, high-growth organizations. Culture is often described as the *way we do things around here*.

Capital Access and Risk

Ask any entrepreneur about his or her greatest challenge, and the conversation will likely turn to capital or how that person funds his or her business idea or venture. Finance is the lifeblood of every company. For new firms, capital is especially critical. This section explores the nuances of accessing and raising funds necessary to start, scale, or grow a venture.

Innovation Strategy and Systems

Innovation initiatives frequently fail and lack sustainability. Why is it so hard to build and maintain the capacity to innovate? The problem with innovation improvement efforts is rooted in the lack of an innovation infrastructure and strategy. Here, we delve into what that means and how organizations can use it to their advantage.

Marketing Strategy and the Customer

Marketing programs, though widely varied, exist to convince people to try or keep using particular products or services. Business builders should carefully plan their marketing strategies and performance to keep their market presence strong. Inventory critical success factors to get a look at the good, the bad, and the ugly of marketing initiatives.

Mentoring and Coaching

Coaching and mentoring can provide various benefits for organizations of all sizes, especially small businesses. When conducted in an efficient and productive manner, mentoring and coaching provide entrepreneurs and business builders a way to connect, learn and grow. Gain insight into what it takes to be mentored and be a mentor. Learn about the important differences between coaches, consultants, and trusted advisors.

People and Talent

Automation and robotics haven't yet fully replaced humans. People remain the fuel for innovative, small businesses, and entrepreneurial ventures. An organization is only as good as its people. How then do you assemble and maintain a quality team, regardless of your industry? Here we take a look at what it takes to attract and retain talent in the twenty-first century and the related challenges in dynamic entrepreneurial enterprises.

To gain maximum value and impact from this book, please watch for these sections in each topical area and apply them to your professional and personal life:

Big Ideas & Reflections

The Big Ideas & Reflections at the beginning of each topical area provide some general observations and frameworks for discovery and self-assessment. Dig deep to find connections and insights by connecting your dots.

Insights Dashboard

The Insights Dashboard provides a recap of the thought pause questions posed in each content area. In addition, fieldwork activities attempt to translate key lessons into insights. This dashboard appears at the end of each topical content section. Field work encourages you to seek out people and/or experiences to internalize your key learnings & insights.

Topical Areas

Topical Areas : Suggested Reading

Charlie "Tremendous" Jones said, "Leaders are readers."[2] He was right. Knowing that most people are too busy to read an exhaustive collection of books, listed below are two highly recommended must-read books for each of the topical content areas of this book. These will provide deeper insights into the topical area and challenge your thinking about your core principles and practices.

Topic	Book Suggestions	Author
Failure Savvy	*The Other "F" Word: How Smart Leaders, Teams, and Entrepreneurs Put Failure to Work*	Dr. John Danner
	Grit: The Power of Passion and Perseverance	Angela Duckworth

---

[2] Charlie Tremendous Jones, **Life is Tremendous**, Executive Books, Mechanicsburg, PA © 1981.

Topic	Book Suggestions	Author
Leadership and Culture	*Good to Great: Why Some Companies Make the Leap and Others Don't*	Jim Collins
	Creating Magic: 10 Common Sense Leadership Strategies from a Life at Disney	Lee Cockerell
Capital Access and Risk	*A Practical Guide to Angel Investing: How to Achieve Good Returns*	Dr. Steven A. Gedeon
	Angel Investing: The Gust Guide to Making Money and Having Fun Investing in Startups	David S. Rose
Innovation Strategies and System	*The Game-Changer: How You Can Drive Revenue and Profit Growth with Innovation*	Alan G. Lafley
	Blue Ocean Strategy, Expanded Edition: How to Create Uncontested Market Space and Make the Competition Irrelevant	W. Chan Kim & Renee Mauborgne
Marketing Strategy and The Customer	*Start with Why: How Great Leaders Inspire Everyone to Take Action*	Simon Sinek
	The Lean Startup: How Today's Entrepreneurs Use Continuous Innovation to Create Radically Successful Businesses.	Eric Ries
Mentoring and Coaching	*The Dream Manager*	Matthew Kelly
	The Coaching Habit: Say Less, Ask More & Change the Way You Lead Forever	Michael Bungay Stanier
People and Talent	*Topgrading, 3rd Edition: The Proven Hiring and Promoting Method That Turbocharges Company Performance*	Dr. Brad Smart
	Startup CEO, + Website: A Field Guide to Scaling Up Your Business	Matt Blumberg

Topic 1

Failure Savvy

I think it's important to have a good hard failure when you're young. I learned a lot out of that. Because it makes you kind of aware of what can happen to you. Because of it I've never had any fear in my whole life when we've been near collapse and all of that. I've never been afraid. I've never had the feeling I couldn't walk out and get a job doing something.

—Walt Disney

It's no secret that our worst fear is often failure. But what if failure was actually a good thing? How do we avoid allowing the fear to cripple people and organizations? Learn about the causes, attitudes, circumstances, and lessons surrounding failure.

Big Ideas and Reflections

Failure is not an easy thing. For some, it is a rite of passage and often reflective of a trait of serial entrepreneurs. For others, failure results in giving up or not trying again.

Assess yourself on the following traits: true talent (it is in your DNA!), talent, and needs improvement. Can you identify an example or situation where you demonstrated this talent? Can you identify a step or several steps to how you might improve on this failure-savvy trait?

Trait	True Talent	Talent	Needs Improvement
Resilience			
Adaptiveness			
Perseverance			
Courage			
Humility			
Intellectual Curiosity			
Confidence			

What's your biggest "successful failure"? Which successful failure are you most proud of in your life? What did you learn from it? What would you do differently if you could do it again?

Who do you look up to that has failed in some aspect of his or her life? What did you learn from that person's failure?

In a commencement speech, Steve Jobs said, "You can't connect the dots looking forward; you can only connect them looking backward." How can you grow and learn from your mistakes? What dots can you connect, and what does it tell you?

On Grit

In business, so much of our success hinges on good connections and a strong network of support, among other things. However, grit is an internal quality and not something bestowed on a privileged few. People from the most modest means or dire circumstances can have grit. It doesn't discriminate based on socioeconomic status, skin color, or gender. Anyone can be gritty.

Omer Shai, the chief marketing officer of Wix.com, said it best in an *Entrepreneur. com* article: "Starting something isn't enough. The ability to persevere and be resilient after that something has been started is the true stamp of an entrepreneur. It's the people who stay the course and continue to invest in developing their enterprise beyond the starting point that should be the model for successful entrepreneurship."[3] Resilience, adaptiveness, perseverance, and courage (one of my favorite words) are proxy words for grit.

Shai makes an important observation when he talks about the necessary conditions for going beyond the starting point. The challenge is that, unlike interpersonal skills, grit is a difficult thing to practice or affect. There aren't many good exercises to flex your grit muscle. It's more of a case of experiences happening to you that require you to adapt and adjust—and thus become grittier.

If you're looking for a real-life example of grit, look no further than Angela Lee Duckworth's studies. As a math teacher at a New York public school, Duckworth was drawn to study the differences between high- and low-performing students. Her strongest performers didn't necessarily have the highest IQ scores, while the so-called "smart" kids weren't always consistent. She started to question IQ as a major metric for success. Later in her work as a psychologist, Duckworth studied various demographics—West Point cadets, new teachers, and salespeople, for example—and drew the conclusion that grit is a major predictor of success. Her work suggests that grittier students are more apt to graduate. In a way, her study of grit has challenged traditional norms about academic performance. Imagine what that might mean

---

[3] Amy Rose. **Why Grit May Be Everything for Success**. Entrepreneur.com (https://www.entrepreneur.com/article/247840)

for the business world … and beyond. If grit is a trait you want to further develop, there are a few things you can do to teach this characteristic to yourself.

- **Manage your distractions.** Identify distractions and set up measures to manage temptation. In those moments of weakness, remind yourself of the reason you started.

- **Change your mindset.** Success is earned. If you desire it, you must work for it.

- **Confront your fears of failure.** If something is worth your blood, sweat, and tears, get comfortable with some amount of failure.

- **Develop a rewards system.** You know what they say about eating an elephant. If you break a goal into smaller pieces and reward yourself along the way, you will be more motivated and feel accomplished.

Thought pause: *Who and what in your life is gritty? What can you learn from their behavior?*

On Honesty

If you want a sense of how important a brand's promise is and how fragile it might be, consider the controversies associated with The Honest Company Inc. as a cautionary tale. The consumer products start-up was initially pitched as an alternative to traditional chemical-heavy products on the market, such as laundry detergent.

Yet, The Honest Company wasn't so honest after all. The eco-friendly claims were exposed in 2016 as less than truthful in a *Wall Street Journal* exposé. What followed was a major product recall and legal trouble. The company ended up reformulating the product in question, but no doubt, the company lost credibility with health and socially conscious consumers who realized The Honest Company wasn't very honest.

To add insult to injury, imagine the backlash when founder Jessica Alba announced that it would replace its CEO with a former Clorox executive. The image Alba worked so hard to create was quickly eroded by the decision. No doubt in some consumers' minds the company (and Alba) had *sold out*.

There are a few lessons here you can apply to any business:

- **Deliver on your promises.** The Honest Company is an egregious example of what happens when you veer off course. For example, if you claim to offer organic, GMO-free products, then offer them. If you are less than genuine, customers will notice, resulting in negative repercussions to your bottom line. In the end, failing to deliver on your promise hurts your organization (and the stakeholders involved, such as employees, suppliers, and communities) just as much as the customer.

- **Don't try to be everything to everyone.** Find what you do. Do it well. There's a lot to be said for specialization.

- **Surround yourself with people of integrity.** After all, you become like the people you spend the most time around.

Thought pause: *Think of a time when you were less than honest in a personal or business situation. What did you learn from the experience?*

On Success

Owning a small business isn't for everyone. It can be an isolating and thankless job. It can mean little sleep and slow growth. However, those who manage to succeed usually do so because they've been intentional in their approach. Here's what I believe sets the winners apart:

- **They think bold.** Another word for this is *courage*. It takes grit to start and continue pursuing a venture. Courage means having a goal and a willingness to overcome adversity to achieve it. To truly create a company of enduring value and one with heart, a goal must be more than financial windfall. Otherwise, you will easily become discouraged because most new businesses are not profitable for a few years.

- **They see the big picture.** Ever heard the expression "Done is better than perfect"? There is a lot of truth to this in the business world. Many "would-be" entrepreneurs are so concerned with getting the timing just right that they never actually get started. No matter how much analysis you put in, there will never be a "right" time. No formula or chart can tell you when to start. It's more of a Nike "just-do-it" approach than a mathematical calculation.

- **They surround themselves with trusted advisors and mentors who can make them better—but not just any mentors.** You need to be careful in selecting whom you seek for advice. Otherwise, you may listen to those who feed your fears. They won't allow you to move past them; thus, you remain stagnant. Instead, you have to be open to hearing out people who question your viewpoints and practices. Growth can often come from a place of challenge.

- **They are selective about who they let in.** Exercise caution when it comes to selecting business partners and vendors. It's important that those in your professional network support your goals and that integrity enters into the equation. Character and moral fiber matters. Will they stand by you in moments of adversity? Do they add value to your skill set? Are they a poster child for your brand?

- **They know how to exercise control (that is, they have high emotional intelligence).** Maintaining proper control means staying true to your vision and trusting your gut in decision-making. You know your business better than anyone else. That means you should be the one calling the shots—not some third-party "expert." After all, your business is your baby, and you wouldn't trust just anyone with your baby, would you?

Success is in reach if you're willing to put in the effort. The story behind Starbucks is a fine example. Following a trip to Italy, Howard Schultz had an idea for upscale espresso cafes like he experienced there. His employer at the time didn't want to expand into owning coffee shops, but they agreed to bootstrap Schultz's venture. They even sold him their brand name: Starbucks.

Thought pause: *What's one thing you can do today to be more successful tomorrow? How will you make that happen?*

On Gender Equity

What does it take to succeed as an entrepreneur? While it's true that more women than ever are working outside the home, they are underrepresented when it comes to business ownership. Why is this the case?

First, women are often met with static when they seek financial and social support for their ventures. It may be a self-fulfilling prophecy. Investment firm Female Founders Fund released a report that underlines this reality. Of the more than two hundred Bay Area start-ups that in 2015 received a financing round of between $3 million and $15 million led by an institutional investor, a mere 8 percent were led by women. This was a decline of nearly 30 percent from the previous year.

Second, women may be discouraged from even considering the option of entrepreneurship in the first place because they feel it is not obtainable. Consider it a chicken/egg phenomenon. There are 7.8 million women-owned businesses across the United States, which is 28.7 percent of the total business establishments. More women might feel empowered to start a business if they saw others out there doing the same thing and had the peer-to-peer learning and network support of their male counterparts.

Some women go out on a limb and blaze their own trails. Sandra Lerner cofounded Cisco with her now ex-husband in 1984. They saw a need and developed a solution that is ubiquitous in office environments today: a router. Following this success, Lerner went on to codesign Urban Decay, a cosmetic company known for its bold colors, which later sold to L'Oréal.

Why can't there be more Sandra Lerner's in the world? When you consider that women make up more than 50 percent of the population, our collective goal should be to make sure this percentage is representative of the number of women-owned businesses. Why? *because by addressing the entrepreneurial gender gap, we could address a significant component of why our economy has been stuck in low to no growth mode.*

According to a Boston Consulting Group Study, if women and men participated equally as entrepreneurs, global gross domestic product could rise by as much as 2 percent or $1.5 trillion. So now that we've established that the playing field needs some leveling, a few questions arise.

Can we work to overcome these misperceptions as a society? If so, how? To answer that, let's look at a few positive steps we can take:

- We can encourage discussions in classrooms about history's standout women entrepreneurs. Aspiring woman-owned businesses need role models and mentors. It is shameful that entrepreneur is not a career included on the PSAT career wheel. It should be.

- We can tell the stories of women who have started, launched, and grown successful high-performance Inc. 5000 or Fortune 1000 companies.

- We can support entrepreneurial education and assistance programs (financially and relationally) like our NIIC WEOC (Women's Entrepreneurial Opportunity Center), which is working to reduce the major barriers and obstacles I discussed in the Foreword to this book.

- We can pay it forward—be a mentor, trusted advisor, advisory board member, angel investor, or sounding board for women-owned businesses.

The good news is that the more we celebrate and highlight women entrepreneurs, the more our culture will change. The media as a whole may take note and (hopefully) tell their stories.

Thought pause: *What female business owners in your community do you admire? How can you support their personal and professional growth? What can you learn from their experiences and their personal story?*

On Resilience

According to the US Bureau of Labor Statistics, about 50 percent of all new businesses survive five years or more, and about one-third survive 10 years or more. The US Small Business Administration (SBA) cites 34 percent of all businesses started will close in the first two years of operation. So why would anyone in their right mind start a company? No business owner starts a venture with the intention of failing. Entrepreneurs are "all in." Failure is not an option, or so they think. But sometimes failure is inevitable. When it happens, it can be a chance to pause and reflect on what you can do differently next time and increase your odds of a successful second, third, or fourth venture.

Successful companies and their leaders understand that failure is part of the game yet don't let the possibility cripple them. The Steve Jobs' story of resilience is instructive for how to overcome failure and rejection. His forward-thinking design decisions were not initially well received at Apple. He went on to hone them at NeXT and Pixar. He returned to Apple with winning designs for the iMac, iPod, iPhone, and iPad. Jobs never gave up, and that's what resiliency is all about.

Like Jobs, there are several practical ways you can use failure to your advantage and to identify it as Professor John Danner, author of *Failure: The Other "F" Word* calls it, "a strategic resource."

- **Channel your emotions into something positive.** You have two choices at this juncture: wallow in self-pity or proactively start fleshing out your next big idea. Find a way to transfer that nervous energy into motivation and don't waste precious time and emotional capital. Smart and savvy entrepreneurs are adaptive, iterative, and reflective.

- **Don't forget about passion.** You're far more likely to succeed if you pursue a concept you love. After all, you must sell yourself first on the product or service before you can get customers on board. Fun is underrated. If you had little or no connection to your original concept, then maybe it's time to explore something that creates a visceral response this time around. Smart and savvy entrepreneurs are passionate, intellectually curious, and determined.

Entrepreneurs have resilience in their DNA. Take it from Sir Richard Branson, founder of the

Virgin Group, who said: "You don't learn to walk by following the rules. You learn by doing, and by falling over." Resilience means staying in the game, even when it's most inconvenient.

Sometimes you have to remove all emotion from the situation and look at it from an outsider's perspective. For example, you might consider where things didn't happen the way you anticipated they would. Feedback from customers? Production costs too high for a likely sale price of the product? What commercialization derisking needed to happen but didn't? Once you have this intelligence, you can turn around and create something bigger and better next time around.

Smart and savvy entrepreneurs see around the corners, connect disparate dots, and possess incredible emotional intelligence, self-awareness and self-control. Remember, failure is a natural part of life—and business. The sooner we lean into failure, the better off each of us will be.

Thought pause: *Think of a recent business failure. How will the lessons make your business stronger? What false-starts have you experienced? How did you overcome adversity?*

On Expertise

Today, people won't take you seriously unless they perceive you as someone who knows your stuff. *But how do you become an expert in the first place?* The short answer is this: It's an ongoing process. It requires intense focus, dedication, and a variety of market-smart strategies. Experts, then, are self-made. Even Winston Churchill, known to be a great communicator, practiced his delivery in front of a mirror. How then is an expert made? Consider these 5 actionable tips:

1. **Build and establish credibility by writing for industry publications.** It's now easier than ever to find publications looking for new content. Content is king, after all. A good launching pad is to secure a spot as a guest author in niche industry blogs. This will help you build some momentum and confidence so you can later pitch to larger publications. Make sure your articles are timely, relevant, and on point for the subject matter.

2. **Publish a book.** The internet is the great democratizer when it comes to publishing. Self-publishing is easier now than ever. Writing a book (or e-book) can give you the leverage you need to impress or influence clients, vendors, and others. It is a terrific tool for differentiating yourself.

3. **Speak at industry events/offer workshops.** Do your homework by seeking out the types of events your ideal clients would attend. Make it a point to hone your public speaking skills so your *storytelling* can connect deeply with your audiences. If this isn't second nature to you, you might consider joining a Toastmaster International Club to build confidence and gain feedback in a nonthreatening setting.

4. **Focus on the details/carve your niche.** Autograph your work with excellence. Produce good work consistently (go above and beyond in delivering value) and on time. Then, people will want to keep working with you. Your reputation will precede you, in a good way. Lee Cockerell, former executive vice president for Walt Disney World, once said, "Every leader is telling a personal story about him or herself by his/her actions, what story are you telling?" Be sure to know what you want to be known for and what you believe you and your company do better than anyone else. What's your secret sauce?

5. **Land high-profile clients.** It only takes one big-name company to change your company's trajectory. Don't be afraid to think big and approach a company outside your comfort

zone. The right reference clients can make all the difference in your success or failure in an industry segment or in a niche area of expertise. Sometimes you have to leave a sixty-mile radius of where you live to be considered an expert.

If you are disciplined, consistent, and committed, the rest will follow.

Thought pause: *What's your area of expertise? What steps can you take to further develop your craft? How can you monetize your expertise or thought leadership into a business venture? Which of the 5 actionable tips have you accomplished or attempted? What were the results?*

Failure Savvy

Insights Dashboard

Topic	Thought Pause	Insights/Field Work
On Grit	Who and what in your life is gritty? What can you learn from their behavior?	Interview someone with grit. What gives that person gravitas or presence? What did you admire most about this person?
On Honesty	Think of a time when you were less than honest in a personal or business situation. What did you learn from the experience?	Think about a difficult situation you had to confront. Did your actions pass the mirror test?
On Gender Equity	What female business owners in your community do you admire? How can you support their personal and professional growth? What can you learn from their experiences and their personal story?	How can you augment more inclusiveness in your decision-making process? Can you create a safe environment for it?
On Resilience	Think of a recent business failure. How will the lessons make your business stronger? What false-starts have you experienced? How did you overcome adversity?	Who do you admire that failed? What can you learn from their example? How did they pick themselves up? Inventory your personal values around failure. Interview a serial entrepreneur and learn about his/her successes and failures.
On Expertise	What's your area of expertise? What steps can you take to further develop your craft? How can you monetize your expertise or thought leadership into a business venture? Which of the 5 actionable tips have you accomplished or attempted? What were the results?	What is your passion? What can you be excellent at doing? What word or words best describe you as a brand? What lifelong learning opportunities would you like to take advantage of? What holds you back from doing so?

Topic 2

Leadership and Culture

In our early years, we didn't talk about culture much. We hadn't documented it all. We just built a business that we wanted to work in. And, that was great. But the real return on culture happened when we started getting more deliberate about it. By writing it down. By debating it. By taking it apart, polishing the pieces and putting it back together. Iterating. Again. And again.

– Steve Jobs

Culture is a buzzword we encounter almost every day. But what do we really mean when we say this? What factors contribute to a positive culture? How can leaders infuse a culture into their organization's DNA? In this section, we examine the intersection of leadership and culture—and what it means for high-potential, high-growth organizations. Culture is often described as the "way we do things around here."

Big Ideas and Reflections

All organizational problems are leadership or people problems. This is the Reader's Digest summary of one of my favorite graduate school classes in organizational development.

Assess yourself on the following leadership traits (True Talent—Talent—Needs Improvement). If you could pick one role model or leader you most admire, who would it be? What leadership style do you most follow? In what area are you holding yourself back in your leadership talent?

Trait	True Talent	Talent	Needs Improvement
Lifelong Learner			
Visionary			
Level 5 Leadership: Humility + Will*			
Change Agent			
Confidence			
Self-Awareness			

Culture is the work of the leader. It can't be delegated. Culture is often defined as "the way we do things around here." There are many potholes in culture building.

Examine the following potholes:

--Organizational lack of trust,
--Lack of candor, lack of trust in the leader,
--Lack of retention of your talent, or
--No constructive dissent (everyone agrees with everyone else).

What gets in the way most of your success in your organization? Does your organization have a culture problem?

*Level 5 Leaders <u>https://www.managermentstudyguide.com/leadership_basics.htm</u>

- The first step is their ability to identify and *include the right people* with them toward achieving goals.

- They also do not shy away from *facing and accepting brutal truths* and realities of data, numbers, and situations and at the same time do not lose hope of a better future.

- They also strive toward aligning consistent efforts toward a goal. Rather than giving one massive push, they believe in small but firm pushes to bring in the momentum.

- They also exercise their judgment to understand an aspect, in depth and thoroughly, rather than burdening themselves with myriad information.

- They practice and encourage a disciplined approach toward their work life and as visionaries use carefully identified technologies to give their businesses strategic advantage.

On Cultural Dysfunction

Say what you will about Uber and its founder and former CEO Travis Kalanick, but one thing experts agree on is that this company was innovative in its vision and its business model. The tech start-up was founded with a goal of bringing people together and connecting cities. Nothing had been done on that scale previously. Look no further than its mission: "to make transportation as reliable as running water, everywhere, for everyone." Pretty innovative, right?

The problem is that his vision was drowned out by numerous scandals, controversies, and questionable business practices before a shareholder revolt. Kalanick was personally involved in a number of public displays of poor judgment and leadership.

I don't intend to spur debate or analysis as to whether any of his actions were justified. I think it is clear they were not. I raise these points because I think it illustrates what can happen to a good business model when leadership fails. An innovative vision can only go so far if the people at the top are failing. One of my graduate school professors once said, "Organizations mirror the dysfunction of their leaders." She hit the nail on the head!

What can entrepreneurs learn from this situation?

- **Lesson 1.** Culture is largely driven by the tone at the top. Not many people I know want to work in a toxic culture or for a toxic leader. Top leaders set the ethical climate and guiding values for an organization. When an organization sets and manages people by the wrong targets, it drives the wrong behaviors.

- **Lesson 2.** Uber is a wake-up call from the father of management Peter Drucker, who opined, "Culture eats strategy for lunch." So, even if you have a great strategy, if the culture isn't right, it will not matter what direction or vision you might have. While Uber is only about seven years old, culture runs deep. Changing it will require new levels of transparency and authenticity, new leadership (this alone is insufficient to change culture), and discovering what Jim Collins calls getting your core values right. Culture and strategy are linked and aligned. When they are disconnected, it results in companies making poor choices. This is clearly the case at Uber.

- **Lesson 3.** Leadership can be cultivated. Very few people are born with natural leader qualities. Leaders are self-made, willing to learn, vulnerable, humble, want to be coached, and have high levels of self-awareness. Leadership is not positional or hierarchical. I believe that with high levels of emotional intelligence, time, and experience, ordinary people can rise to greatness.

Thought pause: *Lee Cockerell, former executive vice president of worldwide operations at Walt Disney World once observed, "Every leader is telling a personal story by his or her behavior. What story do you want to tell?"*

On Habits

You don't have to wait for a new calendar year to start working on a new habit. Despite popular beliefs, important and non-routine habits take a lot longer than 21 days to form. In fact, a significant behavioral change takes, on average, 66 days[4] even with some false starts. But what is behavioral change? Behavioral change is a function of your awareness of the need for behavioral change, your willingness to make a significant behavioral change multiplied by the burning platform for change (either a big opportunity (like a promotion or raise) or a big consequence of not changing – like you are going to get demoted or fired.

Consider adopting these five habits of innovative business leaders:

- **Embrace Level 5 leadership.** You've likely heard of emotional intelligence and its application to the workplace. Leaders with high EQs (emotional intelligence) know how to keep their egos at bay. An innovative leader is open to hearing ideas that might challenge their beliefs or the status quo and, in the process, improve or strengthen the idea. (See page 32 for more information on the Level 5 leader.)

- **Don't lose sight of the big picture.** What if Henry Ford had given up after the first prototype? Innovators dust themselves off and see failures as temporary hurdles. Distinguish between activities and results. My first boss told me, "Results, not effort, get rewarded." Be vigilant in keeping score but don't be confused by being busy on your to-do list at the expense of getting the right things done.

- **Listen more, talk less.** When someone is speaking, are you truly listening or busy formulating your response? We are all guilty of the latter from time to time. Good listeners are fully present and know how to make others feel validated and heard. This is critical to team building and personal trustworthiness. Be present and engaged in your relationships with others.

---

[4] https://jamesclear.com/new-habit

- **Stay hungry—for information and meaning.** Innovators are continuous learners. They are often voracious readers and jump at the opportunity to attend a workshop or professional development seminar. Get in the groove—establish some discipline and rhythm in your daily active learning.

- **Connect the dots—it's all about the business model.** Some of the most successful entrepreneurs have multiple and diverse streams of income. Innovators tend to get bored easily, which is why giving yourself some variety in creative pursuits is good for your headspace. Plus, it expands your knowledge base and overall business savvy.

Thought pause: *Which of these habits are you willing to incorporate into your daily routine? If you have already embraced one or several, how has it served you and your business?*

On Intentional Culture

There is a reason cool companies like Starbucks and Zappos get a lot of press. They have made it a point to form and maintain distinct corporate cultures. You might set out with initial ideas in mind about what that entails. But how do you maintain said culture through periods of growth?

Here are a few best practices:

- **It starts with robust employee selection.** The best employers are ones who select employees and do not hire employees. Engagement studies show that most people go to work each day not engaged and inspired by what they do. Sure, everyone needs to put bread on the table, but you don't want to attract a type of person who just shows up solely for a paycheck. In your interviewing process, you should include behavioral-based questions, psychometric assessments that get to the core of their intentions so you can weed out candidates that might not be a strategic fit.

- **It requires constant culture building and ongoing reinforcement of vision, values, priorities, and celebrations of successes.** Exceptional companies that do a great job of culture building work at it. They have discipline, consistency, and a working business model around culture. As companies grow and change, measuring employee engagement, celebrating the wins, and stretching people and the organization's capabilities will be critical to ongoing assessment of culture-building activities. (A simple tool to do so is the Strength of the Workplace.) See: https://q12.gallup.com/Public/en-us/ Features

- **It demands strategic investment in your employees (especially your front line) and alignment of incentives and recognition systems.** Professional development (internal and external) is one way to get everyone on the same page when it comes to your vision and goals. The NIIC works with clients to help analyze, plan, develop, and acquire the talent of the founders and the team. It has many components and can be addressed in many ways. The required talents of the team are also constantly changing based on the phase of venture development. The NIIC uses psychometric assessments like Predictive Index and Gallup BP-10 to help determine and address conflicts or potential relationship issues between founders and owners before they fully materialize in the workplace.

Thought pause: *Have you had experience maintaining your company's culture? What actions did you take to do so?*

On Parenting/Management Style

If you want to raise well-adjusted children who thrive in the workplace, the results of a study might be of interest. The study, published in the journal *Human Relations*, found that the way your parents treated you as an infant—whether they let you cry it out or rushed to comfort you—*influences your workplace behavior and relationships today*[5].

Researchers believe this is because babies whose parents were particularly attentive tended to look at them as a source of support, while those with parents who let them cry did not have the same association. As they grew up, those individuals brought this same mode of thinking into the workplace. Case and point: Those who didn't view parents as a source of support were found to be anxious or avoiding attachment. They tend to manifest fears that people won't return their affection and often overreact anytime they feel their relationships are in jeopardy. They often use guilt and emotional manipulation in hopes that others will stay near and reassure them.

The study also looked at management style and found that anxiously attached people are affected the most by the type of boss they have. When they work for supportive leaders, they have no problems. However, when they work for distant, unsupportive bosses, they do not have positive outcomes. That's because they feel threatened, and their anxieties are often manifested in an unhealthy way.

So, keep in mind the following:

- We each have to assume responsibility and hold ourselves personally responsible for our choices and actions.

- To achieve personal and lasting change, we must be aware of the need for change, possess the willingness to change, and have a burning platform for the change.

---

[5] http://journals.sagepub.com/doi/abs/10.1177/0018726716628968

- Trust (faith in others versus strong personal bonds and feelings for another person) is the key to healthier and lasting organizational relationships. Some followers need constant reassurance from their leaders to more fully contribute in the workplace. Knowing this fact can help supervisors deliver the trust and support necessary to bring out the personal best in others.

- The study findings have tremendous implications for job redesign, selecting supervisors, and delivering quality feedback.

- Issues of workplace performance outcomes and job stress are not unique or specific to millennials. It applies to anyone in the workplace. However, it is clear that by 2025, 75 percent of the workforce will be comprised of millennials.

Thought pause: *For parents, what actions can you take to raise well-adjusted children (and future) employees? For leaders in companies, what steps can you take to become a more supportive leader?*

On Intrapreneurship

Entrepreneurship gets its share of press, but intrapreneurship is its lesser-known relative. I dislike the term *intrapreneurship* and prefer the term *business builder*. Business builders can be growing or building any type of organization—for profit, nonprofit, educational, and government. There is a myriad of reasons why it's important and how it can benefit an organization.

Here are five reasons:

1. **Growth.** The goal of intrapreneurship is to foster an entrepreneurial mindset needed to take growth to the next level. Intrapreneurship does just that by encouraging employees to think beyond the present realities and challenge the status quo.

2. **Innovation.** Without innovation, organizations are stagnant and more likely to tread water and die. Organizations need to be actively innovating all the time. Look at organizations like Apple and Google if you need examples of what I mean. Innovation and intrapreneurship are integral to long-term success. Quite frankly, the top issue keeping CEOs up at night is the pace and rate of innovation in their organizations. Your next big product could be just an idea away. Is your company's climate conducive to innovation, or is it stifling? Remember, innovators come up with ideas. The execution, commercialization, and launch belong to entrepreneurs and business builders who can manage and calculate risk and seize opportunities when others just see problems.

3. **Leadership.** The traits we associate with C-level executives are not necessarily what companies need to innovate. Intrapreneurial leaders have different philosophies, motivations, and preferences that lend themselves to leading growth in product and market initiatives. Intrapreneurship has the potential to engage your best and brightest.

4. **Change.** Many leaders are afraid of change and its consequences. On the other hand, intrapreneurial leaders welcome and seek out change because they know it's a necessary aspect of growth. Intrapreneurial types aren't afraid to ask the tough questions, experiment with different approaches to solve a pain/problem in the marketplace, and pivot to a second or third solution.

5. **Engagement.** Are your employees emotionally checked out or plugged in? Lost productivity can mean slow or no growth. Intrapreneurship, on the other hand, can be a boon to organizations because employees find the projects challenging and meaningful. This leads to higher engagement. Their passion and determination are contagious. As they grow professionally, so does the organization and its opportunities.

Thought pause: *So where does your organization excel and where does it need to improve? What can you do to reinforce a "loose brick" (an area of weakness)?*

Leadership and Culture

Insights Dashboard

Topic	Thought Pause	Insights/Field Work
On Cultural Dysfunction	Lee Cockerell, former executive vice president at Walt Disney World, once observed, "Every leader is telling a personal story by his or her behavior. What story do you want to tell?"	If an extraterrestrial landed at your business, how would it describe the culture it observed?
On Habits	Which of the 5 habits described in this topic area are you willing to incorporate into your daily routine? If you have already embraced one or several, how has it served you and your business?	What new one or two habits would you like to improve? It takes twenty-one consecutive days to build a habit. Consistency is key.
On Corporate Culture	Have you had experience maintaining your company's culture? What actions did you take to do so?	What are your core values? What stories can you tell to illustrate each of the core values?
On Parenting/ Management	For parents, what actions can you take to raise well-adjusted children (and future) employees? For employers, what steps can you take to become a more supportive leader?	What one or two steps can you take to create a healthier environment for your employees or yourself?
On Intrapreneurship	So, where does your organization excel and where does it need to improve? What can you do to reinforce a loose brick (area of weakness)?	How can you spot true entrepreneurs in action in the workplace? What can be done to build a culture that encourages big ideas, game changers, or market disruptions?

Topic 3

Capital Access and Risk

*Risk comes from **not** knowing what you're doing.*

—*Warren Buffett*

Ask any entrepreneur about his or her greatest challenge, and the conversation will likely turn to capital or how that person funded his or her business idea or venture. Finance is the lifeblood of every company. For new firms, capital is especially critical. This section explores the nuances of accessing and raising funds necessary to start, scale, or grow a venture

Big Ideas and Reflections

Forty-one years ago, Apple started in a garage. To generate the $1,350 in capital used to start Apple, Steve Jobs sold his microbus and Steve Wozniak sold his calculator. They didn't have a cap (capitalization) table or turn to outside investors. Instead, they focused on their vision of computing.

You have a one-in-seven chance of obtaining outside funding. This is based on historical yield rates of qualified ventures seeking capital. Recently, a large Indiana-based angel syndicate said it invests in about one out of forty applicants for funding. If you are fortunate enough to secure funding, it doesn't mean you will get all the money you need.

Fewer than 0.7 percent of all small businesses are high performance, often easily qualifying for outside investment. Most of the rest of the early-stage companies are self-funded or bootstrapped.

Assess yourself on your readiness to obtain outside angel funding. If a particular dynamic is a gap/blind spot, more work needs to be done before obtaining outside investment. Be honest and realistic in your assessment.

Early-Stage Venture Readiness Self-Assessment	Yes	No	This Is a Gap/ Blind Spot
The founder(s) is/are serial entrepreneurs.			
The founder(s) is/are coachable and self-aware.			
The founder(s) and team are ready to have a boss.			
The founder(s) has/have domain expertise/industry experience.			
The business venture has paying customers.			
The founder(s) have realistic expectations of their venture's value.			
The founder(s) have leveraged the insights and knowledge of trusted advisors.			

Trusted advisors may include mentors, other initial investors, legal representation, accountant, insurance agent, strategist, banker, and other smart outside resources to make informed decisions about their business venture. ***Who in your life fills the role of a trusted advisor?***

On Early-Stage Investments

The days are gone when a start-up has a 150-page polished and bound business plan. Today, ideas are a dime a dozen. So, unless you have actively engaged in customer discovery and validation activities to find a robust business model to create and capture value, you just have an idea. Furthermore, unless you know your customers' pain or have discovered (and validated) their needs, there really is little chance an outside investor will take you or your venture seriously.

Keep in mind the following early-stage investment basics:

- You only need a business plan if you are raising external capital or applying for a traditional bank loan. For everyone else, an expanded executive summary and some lean canvases with actual field work, experimentation, and customer feedback will be sufficient to get the conversation started.

- Only one in seven early-stage start-ups actually achieve any level of funding for their start-up venture. There better be something unique, special, or different about your business concept or model. Recognize you are competing, and having a good idea is just the admissions ticket; it doesn't get you on the rides. What is your secret sauce?

- The strength and validity of your business model is more important than having a written business plan. Most successful Inc. 500 founders never had a written business plan.

- Thinking and doing, iterating and learning are the business fundamentals your scrappy start-up needs to embrace today.

- Unless you are in an entrepreneurial hot spot—Austin, Cambridge, or Palo Alto—there are more ideas chasing investors than the other way around. However, keep in mind that we still don't have enough entrepreneurs in the world no matter how you slice it.

- Don't use coastal valuations as the basis for a middle-America investment opportunity. It just doesn't work that way. It is unlikely and improbable that your napkin drawing or rough sketch is worth as much as you think it is.

- Be realistic. No one is going to give you a Brinks armored truck of money based on your idea. Your track record, management bench strength, ability to hit milestones, and how you derisk your venture will matter more to an investor than a rosy set of unrealistic, hockey stick financial projections.

Thought pause: *If you own a business, have you thought through whether you want outside investors? If you do, have you considered what it will mean to have a boss?*

On Banking

Starting a small business can be rough, especially when it comes to navigating uncharted territory, such as financing. Here are some important considerations to increase your chance of qualifying for funding or picking the right type of funding to support your business:

- **You might not need bank financing right now.** The most important step in the process is figuring out if you even need to go the bank financing route. For example, you might need a loan for the cost of new equipment, real estate, or expansion. Many banks offer asset-based lending products at attractive long-term rates today. Or you might consider bootstrapping or self-funding. It is used nearly nine out of ten times by early-stage businesses.

- **Keep your options open and flexible.** Securing financing is exciting and essential, but don't get complacent. Instead, be sure to develop contingency plans in case the bank says no or not yet. Know what the bank wants and expects in a business case for funding. Despite commercials on television and in print saying there is a lot of free government money out there, you should remind yourself that there is no such thing as a free lunch. There are US Small Business Administration loan products, and working with a community bank with expertise and volume in underwriting these federal government loans is critical.

- **Obtain expert advice.** Know if what you want is realistic with a bank, or assess whether you would be better served by an angel investor or a customer-funded business deal. Peer to peer lending and online lending platforms through FinTech companies are appearing online everyday disrupting the traditional methods of financing a business and providing a variety of platforms for lending and disintermediation. Complete your due diligence on their product offerings and their value propositions, since many of these entities are not regulated like traditional banks.

Thought pause: *If your business has been funded, what were the biggest obstacles to accessing capital? If you are considering outside funding, have you done a reality assessment of the pros and cons of outside investors?*

On Funding Strategies

It's no secret that starting a business takes money. Even the most straightforward business plan requires some cash, or capital—one of the four pillars of entrepreneurial success. The others are: talent, works paces, and networks. There are, however, ways to start a business with limited resources. Here are three strategies:

1. **Reduce your initial financial needs.** Be market smart and adaptable. Set milestones and stage your growth. Use your profits from your customer contracts or sales to grow your business. Many innovative companies offer professional services and use the profitability from those services to develop their products. Depending on the research study you read, the cost of starting a company today ranges from $30,000 to $90,000. Size your financial commitments to your execution and validation of your business model. Work with knowledgeable entrepreneurial support providers like the NIIC (www.niic.net) to reduce your risks of start-up and increase the likelihood your venture can get off the ground faster and smarter.

2. **Bootstrapping your venture.** Bootstrapping is a fancy word for self-funding your business without the use of third-party investment. Most small businesses start this way. Aspiring entrepreneurs might transition to entrepreneurship while working a day job to ease into the risks and rewards that come with self-employment. Instead of going full-throttle, you might consider testing your minimum viable product to gauge initial demand. Once you start bringing money in the door, you can invest in yourself and piecemeal the business to get it to where you need it to be your sole source of income.

3. **Seek other people's money.** You may not have the cash, but those in your circle might. Don't rule out the possibility of getting help from friends and family. You also might look to angel investors, who are wealthy individuals who back initial business ideas. Similarly, venture capitalists—typically corporations—tend to scout businesses that are already launched. However, the vast majority of ideas and start-ups will not obtain venture capital (VC) funding. In fact, only 1 to 2 percent might be considered. Angel investing isn't easy either. Less than 20 percent of those early-stage companies seeking angel capital will actually receive any. Be sure to seek smart money—an angel with financial

resources and some expertise to help your business (a large contact list or network, domain expertise, or access to services to lower your burn rate.)

Crowdfunding, through venues like Kickstarter, is a social way to fundraise. Don't overlook the US Small Business Administration loan programs operated in conjunction with local community banks. They have loans and grants available to qualified businesses. Last, don't forget about your local bank. A line of credit, working capital loan, or equipment purchase might be a possibility if your finances are in order. (This means you have some assets to pledge and a high credit score.)

Thought pause: *What resources have helped you navigate the choppy waters of financing?*

On Angel Investors

During the last five years, Ralph Marcuccilli has raised nearly $5 million dollars to build his company, Allied Payment. Allied Payment offers online bill payment services to financial institutions, including banks and credit unions as well as directly to consumers. When asked what angel investors in Northeast Indiana look for in investing, Ralph and several of his investors in the room shared the following:

- A committed founder who is personally, financially, and passionately committed to the business and its success. Founders need to be aligned with their investors and have skin in the game. (A significant part of their net worth at risk, regardless of what their net worth is. Ralph is all in and has used his savings to invest alongside his outside investors.)

- Ensure *no* part-timers at the top. You must have a full-time founder or CEO, or the business will never grow and scale.

- Create a robust and proven business model with major recurring revenue and big margins exceeding 30 to 50 percent or more. High margins can often absolve many of the sins in growing a business. Things don't always work the way you planned, modeled, or assumed.

- Surround yourself with credible people who believe in you and who support you by providing access to their established networks and expertise (investors, talent, distribution, customers, and channels).

- Focus on realistic projections of where you are and where you want to go. Sophisticated investors will ask you about your last set of projections and where you are on achieving those business results.

Sometimes, angel investors band together and form an angel syndicate. Keep in mind the following key success factors in launching and managing a local seed fund. Include the following:

1. Creating and validating your investment thesis.

2. Establishing a long-time horizon for results and exits.

3. Delivering education both to politicians and entrepreneurs.

4. Finding appropriate measures of success.

5. Communicating your success stories.

6. Having a firm handle on your community's deal flow for quality venturable business ventures.

Thought pause: *What actions can you take to become more marketable and attractive to outside investors, angel investors, and a financial institution or credit union?*

On Risk-Based Thinking

Despite popular stereotypes of entrepreneurs being huge risk-takers, they are not. Entrepreneurs are calculated or prudent risk-takers. They examine situations thoughtfully and with a critical eye, not impulsively as if they were in Vegas and putting all their money on red in a game of roulette. A successful entrepreneur's perception of risk often from than the actual risk in a situation. Optimistic entrepreneurs may wear rose-colored glasses and mischaracterize or mistakenly assess risks leading to business failure. It is no wonder more than 50 percent of all business start-ups fail in first five years. Undercapitalization is one of the biggest reasons for business failure.

Successful entrepreneurial founders are adept and astute at contingency thinking, seeing around corners and planning scenarios for when their plan A quite doesn't materialize the way they expected. While ideas are a dime a dozen, the execution is what makes the difference between success and failure. Successful entrepreneurs have a plan B and plan C. They are contingency thinkers.

Coachable and self-aware entrepreneurs know the difference between high risk/big bets and lower risk/smaller bets. They surround themselves with people who give them their real, unfettered perspective on what they should do versus surrounding themselves with people who tell them what they want to hear.

Entrepreneurs believe in themselves and their ideas. Smart entrepreneurs are humble and fiercely committed to their passions. Through perseverance and resilience, entrepreneurs work long and hard to advance their dreams and to bring their ideas to life.

Building an entrepreneurial venture is complex and challenging. There is a myriad of commercialization risks that an entrepreneurial founder and team has to manage daily. These may include execution, product, technological, management, financial, operational, and channel risks.

Entrepreneurs view risk differently than the average person. Successful entrepreneurs do not avoid or dodge risk. They mitigate risks, not avoid them. They work hard to overcome threats, adversity, and obstacles in their businesses. Entrepreneurs lean into uncertainty and work with their teams and trusted advisors to manage the outcomes from tenuous situations that often undermine their business venture and its likely success.

While I don't recommend this, consider FedEx. In 1974 they were on the verge of bankruptcy. The founder took the last $5,000 of the company's assets and turned it into $32,000 by gambling in Las Vegas. Today, FedEx is worth more than $30 billion. Who said luck doesn't play a role in a business venture's success? Thinking about luck, Richard Branson speaks about calculated risk-taking. He said, "The luckiest people in business are those who are prepared to take the greatest risks," Branson writes. "We can all create our own luck by taking the necessary risks to open the door to change, progression and success."

Thought pause: *What is the biggest risk you have taken in your life? How did it work out for you? What would you do differently? How risky a person are you? Would others describe you the same way? How do you mitigate risk in your life?*

On Embracing Risk

In business (and life), we often experience times that test our patience and resilience. Sitting out might seem like the safe bet, but the cost of complacency is much higher than the risk of engaging. There is a reason people say adapt or risk becoming obsolete. Successful entrepreneurs are adaptive, intentional, and highly self-aware.

Survival mode is complacency. If your business model hinges on complacency, you're likely "breeding failure," as American businessman and author Andy Grove called it. Instead, be intentional and chart a course. Do you see white-space opportunities? Do you have a destination you are trying to reach? Can you map the road to get there?

In 1952 Harry Markowitz presented an essay on Modern Portfolio Theory for which he also received a Noble Prize in Economics. His theory put forth the idea that risk can be reduced through strong asset allocation of a diversified portfolio of unrelated assets, and an investor's goal is to maximize return for the level of risk taken. Simply put, the higher the potential risk, the higher the expected return. The same is true for our expectation in life and in business; however, it doesn't always work that way! Don't be fooled. Smart business builders are market smart. They are constantly scanning, assessing, evaluating, measuring, and determining what risks are worth the expected return.

If you want to see a classic example of the cost of missed opportunities, recall the downfall of Blockbuster. Instead of seeing the writing on the wall and evolving with technology, it stagnated. By the time the company had come to terms with its failure, the market opportunity had shifted to favor a new business model and approach to solve the pains, gains, and jobs to be done that consumers complained about. Think about it: in the year 2000, Blockbuster had the opportunity to buy Netflix for $50 million and passed up the opportunity. *Imagine what if …?*

An intentional approach, on the other hand, calls for bold moves in the face of adversity and uncertainty. It's an act-now, think-later mentality. I don't mean to discount real externalities like a weak economic outlook, financing issues, or budgeting concerns. Instead, I challenge business owners to remain plugged in to market conditions and maintain a clear vision coupled with agility. Remaining stagnant during an economic downturn can be the kiss of death, while

Karl R. LaPan

making a bold move could mean resounding success. Jack Welch, executive chairman of The Jack Welch Management Institute, always said the best time to grow is when others are contracting or on the sidelines because of the economic climate and uncertainties. History and fortune favor the bold.

Thought pause: *What would happen if you took that risk you've put off? What do you have to gain? Is there an inflection point for you to step out and up while your competitors are tenuous and unsure?*

Capital Access and Risk

Insights Dashboard

Topic	Thought Pause	Insights/Field Work
On Early-Stage Investments	If you own a business, have you thought through whether you want outside investors? If you do, have you considered what it will mean to have a boss?	Do some self-reflection on the fact that if you take any outside funds, you have lost control and have a boss. Are you ready for this reality?
On Banking	If your business has been funded, what were the biggest obstacles to accessing capital?	What one or two things can you do to prepare yourself for meeting with the bank commercial loan officer? Do you want an SBA-backed loan? What will make you more credit worthy (character, collateral, cash flow, etc.)?
On Funding Strategies	What resources have helped you navigate the choppy waters of financing?	What option can be constructed or sensitivity analysis can be performed to best evaluate what strategy benefits you and your venture?

Topic	Thought Pause	Insights/Field Work
On Angel Investors	What actions can you take to become more marketable and attractive to outside investors, angel investors, and a financial institution or credit union?	While the angel investors are interviewing you, you should interview them: How many investments have they made in early-stage companies? How do they mentor and connect the venture with resources? How aligned are you with the investor's thinking and beliefs?
On Risk	What is the biggest risk you have taken in your life? How did it work out for you? What would you do differently? How risky of a person are you? Would others describe you the same way? How do you mitigate risk in your life?	Talk to several different innovators, small-business owners, and entrepreneurs and ask them about how they view, manage, and mitigate risk. What differences do you see in their risk mindset and how they view risk in different situations? Identify for yourself your risk appetite and tolerance level.

Topic 4

Innovation Strategy and Systems

What good is an idea if it remains an idea? Try. Experiment. Iterate. Fail. Try again. Change the world.

— Simon Sinek, Author

Innovation initiatives frequently fail and lack sustainability. Why is it so hard to build and maintain the capacity to innovate? The problem with innovation improvement efforts is rooted in the lack of an innovation infrastructure and strategy. Here, we delve into what that means and how organizations can use it to their advantage.

Big Ideas and Reflections

Peter Drucker said, "Innovation is a change in a dimension of performance." Innovation and newness are infused with many different flavors, such as product, process, customer experience, brand, channel, or business model. Too often, people only think of products as innovative.

Think about where you do your best thinking (on a plane, in the shower, or in a local coffee shop) and when you do your best thinking (time of day, day of week, etc.). Where and when is it? What keeps you up at night when thinking about the survival and growth of your business? What competitor, market disruption, or business trend has the potential to dislocate your marketplace competitive advantages?

You can complete an organizational innovation readiness assessment online at https://hbr.org/2015/11/assessment-is-your-company-actually-ready-to-innovate.

Studies have shown that some of the major barriers/obstacles to innovation in organizations include, but are not limited to:

- Risk-averse culture (favors status quo and tried and true)
- Lack of metrics
- Lack of innovation strategy / new product strategy or alignment with corporate strategy
- Lack of talent / human resources
- Poor communication (between levels of management and across functions)
- Lack of ownership / leadership commitment to follow-through or lack of urgency

Self-assess on the barriers/obstacles in your organization. Which are your biggest roadblocks? Who are the smart people you can surround yourself with to overcome these potential roadblocks or obstacles?

Obstacles	Big Roadblock	Roadblock	Not a Roadblock
Risk-averse culture			
Lack of metrics			
Lack of coherent innovation strategy			
Lack of human resources			
Lack of communications (between functions and management levels)			
Lack of leadership commitment			

On Innovation Districts

One trend that particularly fascinates me is the rise of so-called innovation districts around the globe. Barcelona is considered to be the preeminent with twenty-two. Boston has made headlines with its Seaport Innovation District, the first in the United States. It is estimated that there are now at least ninety of these innovation districts worldwide. Purdue University in West Lafayette, Indiana, is transforming the west side of the campus with a big bet development valued at more than $1 billion.

Although there are no fast and hard rules when it comes to these tech-centric zones, they do exhibit some commonalities. One key point is that they have some association or relationship with a major institution such as a university, hospital, corporation, or research facility. There is an intention of connecting a mix of uses such as commercial, residential, transit, and research and entrepreneurial space, all within a dense urban setting.

The central underlying point, however, is that these spaces are more than a cluster of mere structures. There is so much more than meets the eye. They exist to create an *epicenter that fosters innovation and collaboration* in all its forms.

Here are some key takeaways:

- Like-minded people attract like-minded people, so it's intuitive that innovators want to be around other innovators. These districts equip them to thrive, inspire, and develop to their fullest potential. What was once done in a gated corporate research facility is now done in a more open, public, and collaborative setting.

- Innovation is not something that has to be exercised in a particular venue; we're only limited by our self-imposed restrictions.

- Innovation is a team sport. It is the great equalizer. There is no monopoly on good ideas, but there are advantages that can accrue to smart innovators and entrepreneurs by leveraging entrepreneurial communities like The NIIC or locating in an innovation district.

Thought pause: *If you have visited one of the ninety innovation districts around the globe, what best practices stick out? How can you replicate that success? If you haven't, can you imagine what it might look like in your community?*

On Advancing Innovation

It's no secret that Silicon Valley has long been associated with a hotbed of entrepreneurial activity and innovation. And it's no coincidence that Apple, Facebook, Oracle, Intel, and the like have all come out of this dynamic and innovative geographic area. I believe it's possible for cities of all sizes and types to harness some of that same energy. But how? How can your city become the next cradle of innovation? I believe it comes down to these four factors:

1. **Don't ignore the demographics.** It's no longer just about white, young males and tech start-ups. We need to think well beyond that stereotype and customer segment. According to reports published by Babson College and Baruch College, more than 16 percent of entrepreneurs are first-generation immigrants, and seven out of ten are women. And according to the Kauffman Foundation, one in four new businesses in 2015 were founded by individuals aged fifty-five to sixty-four. While we focus extensively on millennials, we are forgetting these other important groups that have higher new venture start-up rates and higher survivability rates.

2. **Make immersive, experiential entrepreneurship education more accessible and relevant—and support entrepreneurs in all stages.** Small companies grow into larger ones. It's a mistake to only focus energies on established ones. Critical to that growth is access to feeders—entrepreneurial education and expert resources. It is our mission at The NIIC to help turn dreams into businesses. That's why we offer a wide range of programs and services to ventures at all phases of growth. Our new tagline is "Dream big. Get real." Remember, only 2 percent of all US small-business establishments are considered high potential. It really does take a village to build a vibrant entrepreneurial ecosystem, and we should accelerate the growth and development of all interested and motivated entrepreneurs. In 2018, The NIIC launched its new NIIC Navigator™ Learning Management System to make entrepreneurship more accessible and convenient for business builders and entrepreneurs. Our approach was designed to reduce false starts and increase the entrepreneurs' odds of success.

3. **Value and affirm social innovators (problem solvers).** Not all ventures are profit-driven. Some exist for the sole purpose of solving a societal issue or making a social impact. Cities are best served to value this type of thinking and invest resources in them. What

if global hunger could be solved with a social enterprise? Don't underestimate today's social innovators (problem solvers) and their potential for far-reaching impact. Northeast Indiana is blessed with enterprising nonprofit organizations—think about Blue Jacket (hardest to employ), NeighborLink, Easter Seals/ARC, and The League (for the blind and disabled). They are doing innovative and cool things to address social issues in our community with smart business models. What enterprising non-profit organizations are in your community?

4. **Promote an integrative and inclusive approach to entrepreneurship.** Treat entrepreneurs with the same respect as other members of the business community. That means landlords, attorneys, bankers, and other service providers need to level the playing field for entrepreneurs. Entrepreneurs need a supportive community when they are most vulnerable. Entrepreneurs need access to expertise when they have little financial resources to invest. Entrepreneurs need to know it is okay to fail and to start again. As a community, we need to affirm a risk-savvy culture and community commitment to entrepreneurial excellence. Leaning into a failure-savvy and -tolerant culture will lead to more entrepreneurial successes.

Thought pause: *How is your community doing with embracing these points? Where is there room for improvement? Join the entrepreneurial movement and conversation to advance the needs and interests of our country's most valuable assets—business builders and entrepreneurs.*

On Business Models

When most people think about innovation, products are often top of mind. However, an important source of innovation potential is business model innovation. Think about the largest fleet of transportation cars not owning any of its cars: Uber. Think about the largest network of lodging opportunities not owning any of its hotels or resorts: Airbnb. Think about Southwest Airlines flying point to point and only flying Boeing 737 in their fleet when airlines typically ran a hub and spoke system and flew all types of planes. All of these marketplace disruptions reinforce the value and significance of business model innovation. Keep in mind some of these salient best practices for moving your best thinking to the marketplace.

- **Identify likely customer first—discover and validate.** Get out of the lab and get some hands-on customer research to discover and validate the pain, problem, or job to be done. Fast testing of your business concept through customer discovery and validation early can save you time, money, and resources. Using proven, evidenced-based business search methodologies like The SearchLite can save you a lot of heartburn and headaches later.

- **Seek disruption in the marketplace.** Identify the gaps in the existing product or service delivery value chain and create novel or different ways of transforming that product or service to deliver new value to the end user or customer. Think about the pain points and how your solution delivers a better experience, a cheaper product, or a more engaging customer experience (and delight) to a customer segment. Experiment, iterate, learn, and experiment again (and again and again)!

- **Know how your business venture makes money.** The profit model is an essential component to business model innovation. What are the ways you create viable profit streams? Think about the razor and the razor blades. What are your razors and razor blades (annuity streams for ongoing and sustainable profit generation)?

- **Pricing drives behavior.** Think twice about giving something of value away to get initial users. Ash Maurya makes this point very clearly in his book *Running Lean*. Pricing drives behavior. What behavior do you want to drive with your pricing strategy? Think strategically about how best to price and deliver your services.

- **Know and *set* your triggers.** Entrepreneurs often get caught up in loving their idea, product, or service so much that they forget to establish triggers. Triggers are needed to make sure you are not deluding yourself when the market is sending you important feedback. For example, you have a terrific idea for a new product disruption and need to sell sixty-one websites to break even. Establishing specific goals, time frames, and success metrics to help reduce the noise in the marketplace and focus your efforts.

Thought pause: *Sustainable competitive advantage is more than a business concept taught in an MBA class. To achieve it, it takes market focus, discipline, and execution. Where are you lacking, and what can you do to compensate for weaknesses?*

On Product Innovation

Don'ts that may sabotage or highjack your product innovation process—be on guard:

- **Don't operate in silos.** Innovation doesn't belong to a single department, function, or position. It's all around us. Think in terms of big *I* innovation and little *I* innovation. There are different kinds of innovations. And when they all come together toward a focused mission, great things happen.

- **Select vs. settle.** Great people beget great products. While it's tempting to settle for the talent you already have, selecting the right talent is well worth the extra effort. Settling results in subpar performance. Worst yet, putting someone into a role he or she will struggle with is a lose-lose situation. Don't settle—be picky, and you'll come out ahead. Gallup BP-10 and StrengthsFinder and psychometric assessments like Predictive Index can help you maximize each person's potential on your team.

- **Don't believe you always get it right the first time.** You can avoid the high failure rate of innovation by experimentation and iteration. Talk early on with potential customers. Avoid a one-size-fits-all solution. Go beyond the price point. Finally, pick the winning pricing strategy, being conscious of communicating said innovation's value. Remember, pricing drives behavior. What type of behavior do you want to drive with the pricing strategy you implement?

- **Don't fixate on price early on in your market discovery and validation efforts.** Innovation is a nail-biting endeavor in and of itself. Save yourself from unnecessary frustration by knowing if your product is viable for the respective market before going live.

- **Don't assume consumers will buy in right away.** "Build it, and they will come" is not a good philosophy on which to hinge your efforts in product innovation. Take, for example, Google's approach to the development of Google Glass. The tech giant built the product assuming consumers would buy it. As a result, the product flopped. However, had Google developed Glass for the professional and B2B segment, the product might have met a different fate.

Thought pause: *What's one big, huge, gigantic mistake or failure you made relative to product innovation, and what did you learn from it?*

On Entrepreneurial Ecosystems

It's widely understood that the ecosystem (environment, community) in which an entrepreneur is operating (directly and indirectly) affects entrepreneurial success and engagement. But what exactly is such a thing?

Experts, like Dr. Daniel Isenberg, have identified several important domains:

- A conducive culture (e.g., tolerance of risk and mistakes and a positive social status of an entrepreneur).

- Facilitating policies and leadership (e.g., regulatory framework incentives and the existence of tier-one research (R1) universities, federal labs, and corporate research and development).

- Availability of dedicated finance (e.g., business angels, venture capital, microloans); relevant human capital (e.g., top-tier talent, serial entrepreneurs, entrepreneurship educational programs).

- Venture-friendly markets for products (e.g., early adopters for prototypes, reference customers).

- A wide set of institutional and infrastructural supports (e.g., legal and accounting advisers, telecommunications and transportation infrastructure, entrepreneurship promoting associations).

Although they may share some similarities, each entrepreneurial ecosystem is unique and is the result of the hundreds of elements interacting in highly integrated and complex ways. There have been such ecosystems attempted to varying degrees of success around the world, but perhaps the most well-known is Silicon Valley in the United States. Its high concentration of innovative companies, well-educated talent, failure mindset, robust connectors, influencers, and a very well-developed venture capital base has made it the perfect storm of sorts but nearly impossible to replicate elsewhere. The beauty of this is that the six domains (policy, finance, culture, supports, human capital and markets) are strong enough independently, they are mutually reinforcing (See: http://www.oecd.org/cfe/leed/Entrepreneurial-ecosystems.pdf).

Rather than seek what you cannot have or replicate, what if every community tried to become the best version of itself rather than chase other regions' or communities' windmills? Regions need to look at the "native assets of their region and build on those." As Isenberg pointed out, "the drivers entirely depend on and vary according to those parties invested in them."

As for those invested parties, while we can't pick and choose who we work with, we have to meet the entrepreneur, founder, or business builder where we find him or her and the resources to get that individual to the next rung on the ladder of entrepreneurial success. What's quite clear is there is no epicenter or commander in chief of the ecosystem. It is self-regulating and dynamic by definition.

In that same vein, there's no one right way to do entrepreneurship, so the onus rests on each area to invest in the ecosystem that works for us and to engage in one or more of the thirteen elements based on our expertise, passion, and capabilities.

The ecosystem, then, is more than the sum of its parts. To create a culture of entrepreneurship, you have to make entrepreneurship accessible to everyone in the community. If you focus on underserved segments and economically disadvantaged access work and foster success, you will get some high-tech, high-growth companies.

Thought pause: *Where can you play a bigger role in encouraging and nurturing your community's entrepreneurial ecosystem? What can you do to shine a light on the hard work of entrepreneurs versus promoting antiquated entrepreneurial stereotypes?*

Innovation Strategy and Systems

Insights Dashboard

Topic	Thought Pause	Insights/Field Work
On Innovation Districts	If you have visited one of the ninety-plus innovation districts around the globe, what best practices stick out? How can you replicate that success?	What creative ideas/concepts can you take from innovation districts to reimagine your business?
On Advancing Innovation	How is your city doing with embracing these points? Where is there room for improvement? Join the entrepreneurial movement and conversation to advance the needs and interests of our country's most valuable assets—business builders and entrepreneurs.	How do you personally define and measure innovation?
On Business Models	Sustainable competitive advantage is more than a business concept taught in an MBA class. To achieve it, it takes market focus, discipline, and execution. Where are you lacking, and what can you do to compensate for weaknesses?	What are the most unique aspects of the way you go to market and make money? What makes your model unique? How might competitors unravel your marketplace advantages?

Topic	Thought Pause	Insights/Field Work
On Product Innovation	What's one big, huge, gigantic mistake or failure you made relative to product innovation, and what did you learn from it?	How do you incorporate the voice of the customer in your product innovation efforts? What critical success factors influence your product platform direction?
On Entrepreneurial Ecosystems	Rather than seek what you cannot have or replicate, what if every community tried to become the best version of itself rather than chase other regions' or communities' windmills? How can you as a key player make that happen?	Is your ecosystem self-regulating? Where are you most vulnerable in the ecosystem? Where is your community the most unique?

Topic 5

Marketing Strategy and the Customer

Marketing is no longer about the stuff that you make, but about the stories you tell.

– Seth Godin

(Author)

Marketing programs, though widely varied, have an end goal of convincing people to try out or keep using particular products or services. Business builders should carefully plan their marketing strategies and performance to keep their market presence strong and relevant ("Godin's **Purple Cow**"). In this section, we will inventory critical success factors and get a look at and assess the good, the bad, and the ugly of marketing initiatives.

Big Ideas and Reflections

Marketing is focused on understanding and uncovering the wants and unmet needs of the customer. Think about your business's major customer segment groups. How similar or different are their wants and unmet needs? How do your various customer segment groups want your business to communicate with them?

Steve Jobs was a rare and unique entrepreneurial leader. He was a focus group of one. Where do you get your marketing research insights—surveys, one-on-one interviews, focus groups, or something else?

Telling stories and creating emotional connections with your customers are imperative to creating raving fans and lifetime loyalty. What does your business do to connect on deeper levels with its customers? What word or words do you want your business to own when people think about your company? Think Disney and happiness. Think BMW and performance. Think Volvo and safety.

- In his book *It Starts with Why*, Simon Sinek has developed what he calls the Golden Circle, and it has three layers: **Why?** This is the core belief of the business. It's *why* the business exists.

- **How?** This is *how* the business fulfills that core belief.

- **What?** This is *what* the company does to fulfill that core belief.

Check out his Ted Talk online at

https://www.ted.com/talks/simon_sinek_how_great_leaders_inspire_action).

The Ansoff Product-Market Growth Matrix is an excellent tool for cataloging and assessing traditional and non-traditional growth options. In the matrix below, identify key growth strategies for your business in each of these four quadrants:

- **Market penetration strategy.** Existing products and existing markets (selling more existing products to existing customers).

- **Product development strategy.** New products and new markets (replace existing products with something better).

- **Market development strategy.** Existing products and new markets (new geographic markets and opening up new market segments).

- **Diversification.** New products and new markets (could be related or unrelated markets).

		Products	
		Existing	**New**
Markets	**Existing**	Market Penetration	Product Development
	New	Market Development	Diversification

On Finding Your Niche

Food trucks have been one of the fastest-growing food businesses for some time. No longer just a trend in LA or New York, food trucks have enjoyed a loyal following nationwide and in Ft. Wayne for several reasons. It's no accident that food tourism and a food truck culture are permeating our society given some surveys have shown 88 percent of millennials want to explore new types of food. So, I am going to share three lessons you can take from these mobile food start-ups and apply to your business. You may be wondering what food trucks can teach you. Well, this growing, bohemian industry is now at $2.7 billion annually. For comparison purposes, it was 25 percent of this size in 2012. So, the food truck industry can teach us a lot:

- **Think hyperlocal.** The most successful operators know where to go and when to attract business. By analyzing trends, they are able to build and implement a marketing plan. Other business owners can follow suit. Even if your business isn't geographically defined, you can hone in on your target demographic. What are their likes and dislikes? Where do they like to hang out? Who or what influences their thinking? Gleaning such business intelligence allows you to execute your marketing messages with laser-like precision. How can your company and its products/services create a new experience for your clients/customers?

- **Go where the action is on demand in real time.** Whether it's a 5k race, music festival, or other public event, food truck operators can be at the right place at the right time. The mobile nature of a food truck allows for operators to pivot in response to market or environmental forces as necessary. While your business may not be mobile, you can still enjoy similar success. How can you pare it down and hit up the hot spots? For example, if you own a clothing store, maybe you could bring a few top-selling items to a farmer's market or expo show.

- **Find your niche.** All the great food trucks have a unique selling value proposition. It might be eye-catching art or a signature menu item. It could be the way orders are taken or executed. Infusing some personality and life into your brand experience can be key in standing out in a competitive landscape. Your business can learn a lesson or two in this regard. Think beyond your branding when it comes to dazzling the customer. If you have a storefront, what sights, sounds, and smells will they encounter? How can you leave a lasting impression in the consumer's mind?

Thought pause: *Which of these strategies could you adopt and apply to your business? I bet you'll never look at a food truck the same way, will you? What's your most memorable food truck experience? Why was it a "sticky" experience?*

On A Business Name

If you're in the concept phase of your business, then you know that naming your business is a critical step in the development process. After all, the name is often the first impression people have before interacting with your brand.

But where to begin? Here are a few tips to help you get started:

- **It starts with a brand perception.** Start by deciding what images or feelings you want your business to create in the minds of your target audience. For one, the name should reinforce the key elements of your business. Your name should identify your company and its products and/or services. Your customer discovery and validation work, your core purpose (and compelling value proposition), and brand promise will inform this process.

- **Don't be clever when naming.** The more straightforward the name, the less effort you must put forth to explain it. Stay away from the esoteric or overly intellectual. Everyday people can identify with brand names they can relate to and understand. There's a reason companies like Facebook and Lyft have solid name recognition. They call to mind concepts that paint a picture in people's minds. Don't overcomplicate it, or you risk losing your consumer/business focus.

- **Don't be too literal or generic.** It is possible for a name to be too meaningful, however. Avoid geographically focused or generic names. A hypothetical (and fictional) example is Dallas Signs. What if the company wants to expand beyond the confines of the city? How will they forge connections with customers in other cities, states, or countries? Also, what if the company decides to expand its menu of offerings beyond signs? Think about how your name translates into other languages.

- **Think beyond your current situation.** If you are a solopreneur, is there a chance you'll grow the business beyond yourself? Or if you plan to be in business with a partner, what happens if you decide to part ways? It's shortsighted to name the business after yourself or partners.

- **Avoid trends.** Will your business name be relevant in five, ten, or twenty years? The dot-com bubble in the late 1990s serves as a cautionary tale. Then it was considered fashionable to include ".com" after your company name if it was an internet business. Think about the flawed and failed pets.com, eToys.com, and Webvan.com. After the internet bubble burst, this suffix became associated with widespread failure—and who wants that?

- **Lastly, do your due diligence and execute an IP strategy around your potential trademark.** Does anyone own the rights to your potential name? You don't want to face a lawsuit later down the road because you were negligent in this regard. This is when consulting an intellectual property attorney or checking the US Patent and Trademark Office trademark database might come in handy. Also, you should checkout your state's Secretary of State website to do a business search to see if the name is available. In Indiana, go to the Indiana SOS to search a business name.

Thought pause: *If you have successfully named a business, what factors did you consider? In retrospect, what have you learned from naming a business?*

On Strategy

Kids don't take life too seriously, and they also know how to quickly bounce back from adversity. If you've ever seen a lemonade stand enterprise, then you know exactly what I mean. Sometimes the kid behind the stand knows more about how to succeed in business than many adults who tend to overthink things. We all could learn a thing or two from these young entrepreneurs. Here are the three business lessons grown-ups can glean from kids' no-nonsense approach to business:

- **Lesson 1: It's okay to start small.** For many kids, setting up a simple lemonade stand and selling sugary drinks to their neighbors is their first entrepreneurial venture. Talk about modest! But the important point is the fact they started in the first place.

  The lesson here: Don't get overwhelmed by an aspirational goal. Focus on your current strengths and wins. Don't forget the everyday victories that often go overlooked. It's okay to start small—right where you are—and grow from there.

- **Lesson 2: *No* is not the end of the world.** According to J.B. Bernstein, author, motivational speaker, and keynote speaker at one of The NIIC's Ideas @ Work Events, **"No is the beginning of a negotiation."**

  Kids tend to handle setbacks and disappointments differently than adults—and that's usually to their benefit. Lemonade stands aren't always cash cows. Sometimes the weather is bad, or there's competition. While facing setbacks in the business world, look for opportunities to keep propelling forward rather than fixating on a single deal that didn't go well. It's okay to reflect on what went wrong and correct course, but don't obsess—or else you'll do yourself and your business a disservice.

- **Lesson 3: Zero in on your target customer.** For many kids, their first customer will probably be mom, dad, or a sibling. Knowing who is and who isn't your target customer is critical. Finding your desired customer is often the result of rigorous and disciplined customer discovery and validation efforts. Often, this means experimentation and trial and error. Kids learn quickly who the real buyers of their services are. Then, they focus and target relentlessly on that demographic or customer segment.

Thought pause: *Younger people often see the world differently, exhibit vulnerability and demonstrate a willingness to try new things over and over. What other lessons have you learned from younger entrepreneurs? How can you put them into practice in your business today?*

Marketing Strategy and the Customer

Insights Dashboard

Topic	Thought Pause	Insights/Field Work
On Finding Your Niche	Which of these strategies could you adopt and apply to your business? I bet you'll never look at a food truck the same way, will you? What's your most memorable food truck experience?	Share your most memorable food truck or restaurant experience. What made the experience sticky and remarkable?
On a Business Name	If you have successfully named a business, what factors did you consider? In retrospect, what have you learned from naming a business?	Brainstorm some business names and taglines. What one to two words do you want your business to own?
On Strategy	Thinking differently and using lateral thinking can produce different results. What other lessons have you learned from young entrepreneurs? How can you put them into practice in your business today? How, and in what part of your life, might you think differently or laterally to generate new ideas and connect the dots?	Three core strategies are available to every firm: best cost (think Wal-Mart), best price (think Apple), and best solution (think Disney). Which do you want to emulate and why? How can you apply their thinking to your business? What would Sam Walton, Steve Jobs, or Bob Iger do if they ran your business?

Topic 6

Mentoring and Coaching

One of the greatest values of mentors is the ability to see ahead what others cannot see and to help them navigate a course to their destination.

— John C. Maxwell

Coaching and mentoring can provide an array of benefits for organizations of all sizes, especially small businesses. When conducted in an efficient and productive manner, mentoring and coaching provide entrepreneurs a way to connect, learn, and grow. Gain insight into what it takes to be mentored and to be a mentor. Learn about the important differences between coaches, consultants, and trusted advisors.

Big Ideas and Reflections

The Role of Coach

- Sets clear expectations and boundaries with the one being coached.
- Encourages the person being coached to own his or her own outcomes.
- Does not do the work of the person being coached but encourages and pushes him or her to lean into problems and opportunities (accountability partner).
- Focuses on either performance assessment (positive or negative) or personal growth and development.

Important Coaching Skills

- Build rapport (empathy, understanding, and appreciation).
- Ask questions. (What's on your mind? Be sure to ask, not tell, and use open-ended questions.)
- Practice active listening. (Techniques may include paraphrasing, summarizing, repeating meaningful words, questioning, and clarifying.)
- Encourage proactive problem-solving and discovery.
- Give effective feedback (focused on specific behaviors).

Effective Feedback Best Practices

- Should be a gift—show understanding and appreciation.
- Provide a clear expectation of performance.
- Focus on behavior and not the person.
- It should be a tool for continuous learning.
- You can't fix everything so don't overload with excessive feedback (behavioral change).
- Motivate employees to perform better.
- Builds people up from their strengths, not their weaknesses.
- Should not be a surprise to the person receiving it.
- Summarizes and ends on a high note (encouragement).

A technique I have found particularly useful I call the Oreo® cookie feedback approach: Start the session with giving praise (with specific behaviors demonstrated), followed by one area you want the person to strengthen or improve and close with one more layer of praise (with specific behaviors demonstrated.)

Assess yourself on how well you give and receive feedback and your talents as a coach. What "difficult conversations" have you put off having? What holds you back from becoming a "better version of yourself"?

Skill Building	Strengths	Challenges	Comments
Coaching			
Feedback (Giving and Receiving)			

How do you rate on each of the following dimensions? Use the last time you coached someone to higher levels of performance and complete the matrix again for someone whose performance was not up to par. What differences did you observe in your own personal style?

Skill Building	Self-Assessment	Strengths	Challenges
Build Rapport	How were you able to establish trust with the person?		
Ask Questions	What was your question to statement ratio in the meeting?		
Practice Active Listening	How did you para-phrase what you heard?		

Skill Building	Self-Assessment	Strengths	Challenges
Encourage proactive problem-solving and discovery	Did you focus on 1 or 2 specific behaviors that the person needs/wants to change?		
Focus on specific behaviors	Did you give concrete examples to help the person see their behaviors in action?		

On Legacy

If you haven't read Bob Buford's book *Halftime*, you should. Bob states, "The first half (of your life) is busy with 'getting and gaining, earning and learning,' doing what you can to survive, while clawing your way up the ladder of success. The second half of life should be about regaining control, calling your own shots, and enjoying God's desire … for you to serve him just by being who you are, by using what he gave you to work with.' What lies between the two is 'halftime.'"

If you are chasing success, a business builder may be focused on profitability, growing his or her customer base, finding outside investment, or adding new employees or buildings. Essentially, this stage is about keeping score and accumulating stuff.

If you are chasing significance, a business builder may be focused on how he or she is paying it forward or how he or she is making other people's lives better. Essentially, this stage is about surrounding yourself with people who make you better, dreaming big, and becoming the best version of yourself.

If you are chasing legacy, a business builder may be driven to make significant impact. Legacy is about your reputation and what your personal brand promise is to the world and to your family. Across the United States, serial entrepreneurs are transforming communities (Tony Hsieh in Las Vegas and Jeff Vinik in Tampa) to make the world a better place. Essentially, this stage is about following your passion and being part of a greater purpose. In this stage, it is not about you but about the collective us.

Entrepreneurs often feel lonely or isolated. These feelings can lead to anxiety, stress, or abandonment. Entrepreneurs need social interactions and networks that can encourage them, inspire confidence, and provide the emotional support to navigate through the highs and lows of launching and growing a company. Places like The NIIC provide business builders the emotional support system, so they can build their social network, create a sense of connectedness and collegiality to reduce isolation and loneliness, and inspire each entrepreneur to stay committed to his or her business venture. Business builders are courageous individuals and should be acknowledged as such.

Thought pause: *Taking all of this into account, what stage are you in (success>significance>legacy), and how satisfied are you with it? What one choice can you make to lean into what you are chasing?*

On Women Overcoming Imposter Syndrome

Entrepreneurs often suffer from imposter syndrome—and it makes sense. Several national studies of successful people show between 40 to 70 percent feel like imposters at one time or another. In both the research on gender in entrepreneurship and in my interactions with women entrepreneurs (especially when they are thinking of leaving a large, stable employer), they are often told no more times than yes. When this happens, it's easy to doubt one's abilities and to have a self-induced crisis in your confidence levels when the system and the support system appears stacked against you. A key barrier/obstacle identified by our **Women's Entrepreneurial Opportunity Center (WEOC)** is overcoming the confidence gap for women so they start and grow businesses faster.

Here are three ways WEOC and The NIIC work with women entrepreneurs to better build their business and to support self-advocacy:

1. **Lean into pivots.** In many studies of female entrepreneurship, the fear of failure is the top concern of women who launch start-ups. However, pivots are learnings, insights, and aha moments—not failures. They are part of life and business. The problem is that many professional women live in constant fear of failing because of society's negative messaging. But failure in and of itself doesn't define an entrepreneur; it's an opportunity to dust ourselves off and grow.

2. **Be exceptional—and own it.** It's tough to ignore someone who's making waves. Gain positive attention by embracing opportunities, leaning into learning moments, taking calculated risks, and managing uncertainties.

3. **Rise to the occasion.** The next time you feel challenged, remind yourself it isn't just about confidence. Gender doesn't have to define you; your experience, your passion, purpose, and your expertise do. In fact, every asset of your professional life should be a chance for you to showcase your unique talents and gifts. Seize opportunities to assert your entrepreneurial voice by publishing articles, writing op-eds, serving on task forces and boards, and speaking at conferences. In time, your voice and thought leadership will be recognized and sought out as an authority.

The next time you feel a twinge of imposter syndrome, focus on maximizing your strengths and silencing that voice in your head. Also, know that there are resources available, like WEOC, to help you cut through the clutter and boost confidence.

From ideation and start-up through growth and expansion, WEOC was designed to understand and respond to the unique needs of women entrepreneurs. We do this through business growth coaching, training and entrepreneurial education, connectivity, and access to capital.

The NIIC helps you define your unique pathway and then our business coaches orchestrate the resources and connectivity for your venture's success using our proprietary and trademarked Entrepreneurial Pathway—Assess. Discover. Do. ™

Thought pause: *As a female entrepreneur or professional, what strategies have worked for you in overcoming imposter syndrome? Imposter syndrome applies to men, so do any of the three self-advocacy strategies apply in your life? If so, how so?*

On Professional Growth

The one truth people seldom acknowledge is that entrepreneurship and personal/professional growth can be a lonely process. Yes, people are often quick to share success stories, but it's rare to hear about the flops, failures, or false starts. Our society is conditioned for celebrating successes but not embracing and leaning into failure. However, with failure, there is growth, maturation, and savviness!

So, then, whom can a hungry entrepreneur talk to—not only while emerging but also when kicking butt in business? Here are a few ways to push you past your limits:

- **First, schedule meetings with your band of heroes regularly.** If you want to know who the real players are in the business world are, try scheduling an early-morning meeting with someone. Most high-powered people don't have much time to spare during the workday, so they have to start early. So, trade in your midday salad for early-morning eggs and coffee.

- **Second, don't look to one mentor but seek out diverse and contradictory points of views and perspectives.** Many people are inclined to seek the professional guidance of one individual, especially when they are starting out. The reality is that one person's perspective simply isn't enough. You need a team of people and a variety of opinions and life experiences. It is important to know the difference between mentor, coach, and trusted advisor. Test your go-to people against the following trustworthiness definition:

  Trustworthiness is defined as: (Credibility * Reliability* Intimacy) divided by Self-Orientation. The higher the overall number, the higher the trustworthiness. Credibility = how believable the person is; reliability = how likely the person you are interacting will do what they say they will do; intimacy = how strong the mutual relationship is and how invested we are in each other's outcomes; and self-orientation = is the person in it for themselves or for you? Think WIIFM: What's in it for me?

- **Third, there are three leadership behaviors we should emulate in our daily lives to embed and lead.** They are known by the acronym TAC. The *T* is time. How do you as a leader spend your time? This says a lot about what you as the leader value. The *A* is attention. Who and what do you pay attention to as the leader? The *C* is care. What do you as the leader care about? What do you have energy about? Organizations will assess what the leader sustains and shows excitement for over a long period of time.

Thought pause: *What's one thing you can do this week to challenge yourself and advance your community of practice knowledge? How trustworthy are you?*

On Setting High Expectations

I thought I would share **5 life lessons** I learned from my mother. My mom passed away in January 2016 after a twenty-five-year courageous fight with Parkinson's Disease. She was a big role model in my life.

Lesson 1: **My mom taught me to be an inspired & engaged learner**. Several months before she passed away, my mom was working with the nursing home where she resided in Massachusetts to get Wi-Fi and computer stations on her wing of her floor. They had WI-FI on the first floor but not on her floor. She sought out to change the problem that stood in the way of her learning. She wanted to take an online pharmacogenetics course (growing up, she was a nurse and stay at home mom) at the nearby community college. My mom had a 'deal' with me growing up that she would buy me any book as long as I read it and discussed it with her. My mom loved and embraced technology. She was a millennial at heart! She spent years doing and assembling a comprehensive genealogy of her family. There is no greater gift to set you up for life than a love for lifelong learning (being an empowered learner) **and** then doing something with the learning to be relevant and intentional in the world.

Lesson 2: **My mom taught me to advocate for what I wanted.** When I went to my parents in 7th grade, and told them I was bored stiff in public school, and I wanted to go to private boarding school. My father's initial reaction was no way, and my mom went back to work as a school nurse to help pay for my private education. She convinced my dad, and I was off to the best experiences of my life. My mom invested in me and bought into my arguments that I wanted to be in an environment that would stimulate me. She often reflected that this was the best investment she ever made in me because it prepared me so well for life. She sacrificed so I could be inspired and encouraged! I am who I am today because of her.

Lesson 3: **My mom taught me to be generous and caring.** Whether it was helping out at church as a young adult, visiting shut-ins at the local nursing home or in their homes or going door to door with her to educate people on smoking and cancer when she volunteered at the local American Cancer Society, she taught me that I had a responsibility to help others and lift them up. **She taught me that giving my time was the most precious gift I could give**. She loved to educate and share with others. She loved to debate with me politics, sports (she knew a lot more than me on this topic!) and religion. She always asked me more about what

I was doing, and how I was giving back and not as interested in any personal success I might have had along the way as she was the significance and difference I was making in the world. She was intellectually curious, and she was always my best PR agent!

Lesson 4: **My mom taught me to be confident and courageous about my career, life, and parenting choices**. She always focused on my strengths and how to make them better. She never dwelled on my shortcomings. She didn't inspire me by trying to fix me. She worked hard to make sure I was aware of how to become the best of the version of myself. She loved to challenge my thinking. She set really high expectations of what she felt I could do in my life. She always reminded gently but clearly when I fell short of expectations – not in a negative way but in a motivational way. Sometimes my mom might have been hardheaded and would not take "no" for an answer. At one of our annual Ideas@Work events the NIIC hosts to shine a light on entrepreneurship, sports agent, JB Bernstein reminded me that "No is the beginning of a negotiations." As she was failing in recent years, I often had to negotiate with her because her intellectual mind far outpaced what her worn out body would allow.

Lesson 5: **My mom taught me to have a sense of humor**. She never defined herself by the enormous limitations (the physical and emotional toll that twenty-five years of Parkinson's had on her body and her mind) the Parkinson's Disease placed on her life. She never complained –why me or had self-pity. She used her disease to impact others. While many of her friends when she was diagnosed with the disease didn't see it as a real chronic illness - like cancer or heart attacks – or it was an old person's disease (until Michael J. Fox came along) she sought to educate others, motivate others and often knew more about the disease (started a support group, studied and read everything about the disease) than her neurologists or parkinsonologists. She always put others first and loved to share her insights in the nursing home through book club, through programs she ran on Parkinson's and through her art and music talents (none of which I inherited). She had an awesome gift of touching and connecting with other people. After she died, many people, whom I did not know, shared how she impacted their lives.

My mom's life is congruent with an observation made by the Blessed Mother Teresa of Calcutta who said, *"We cannot all do great things, but we can do small things with great love."* It is worth acknowledging that Blessed Mother Teresa was declared a saint in September 2016. She was right about the difference we can each make in our life if we choose to do so.

Thought pause: *What life lessons have impacted you most? What expectations have been set for you? By whom? What specific actions have you taken to aspire higher? What difference(s) do you want to be intentional about making in the next 3-5 years?*

Mentoring and Coaching

Insights Dashboard

Topic	Thought Pause	Insights/Field Work
On Legacy	Taking all of this into account, what stage are you in, and how satisfied are you with it? What one choice can you make to lean into what you are chasing?	Where are you in your life—success, significance, or legacy? What does the next rung on the ladder look like and why?
On Women Seeking Mentors	If you were a female professional seeking a mentor, what qualities do you look for in a mentor?	How can you support building and expanding your inclusive network?
On Professional growth	What's one thing you can do this week to challenge yourself and advance your community of practice knowledge? How trustworthy are you?	What are your plans for the next twelve to eighteen months for lifelong learning and professional development? What credentials, certifications, or degrees are important to you and why? If you could quit your job and do anything you wanted, what would it be?
On Setting High Expectations	What life lessons have impacted you most? What expectations have been set for you? By whom? What specific actions have you taken to aspire higher? What difference(s) do you want to be intentional about making in the next 3-5 years?	Who inspires you and makes you better? Do you seek out people who challenge your thinking and who push you to be uncomfortable? Are you intentional in your relationship seeking? Inventory success practices of others for how you can be a "better version of yourself".

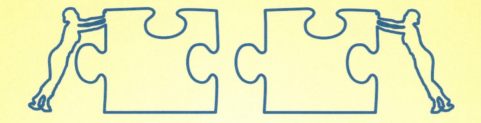

Topic 7

People and Talent

Great vision without great people is irrelevant.

– Jim Collins, *Good to Great*

Automation and robotics haven't yet fully replaced humans. People are still the fuel for innovative small businesses and entrepreneurial ventures. An organization is only as good as its people. How then do you assemble and maintain a quality team, regardless of your industry? Here we take a look at what it takes to attract and retain talent in the twenty-first century and the related challenges in dynamic entrepreneurial enterprises.

Big Ideas and Reflections

Do you have the talent you need to build and grow your organization? What is the quality of your talent (A players to C players) in your organization? How right fit is your talent?

Do you use hiring assessment tools and psychometric assessments like DISC or Predictive Index to identify, recruit, and select talent? The best organizations don't hire. They select talent. How do you select talent? How do you identify high-potential talent in your organization? How do you develop talent?

What attributes do you look for when hiring talent in a high-performance organization? Honesty, hunger to learn, smart, self-aware, coachable, character, humble, resilient, team player, and/or adaptive?

What works well (strengths) and what is not working as effectively as it could (improvement areas) in each of the employee lifecycle process steps. Note below the things that could be leveraged for greater effectiveness, and note the strengths that define your organization's brand and employee experience.

Talent/Human Capital Lifecycle

Process	Strengths	Improvement Areas	Comments
Attraction/ Prescreening			
Recruitment			
Onboarding			
Development			
Promotion and Retention			
Renewal			

On the US Midwest Advantage

So often we associate innovation and entrepreneurship with Silicon Valley or Cambridge start-ups. While both coasts get a lot of press for having dynamic and engaging ecosystems, there's so much more to the entrepreneurial story. But as we know, good Midwesterners just don't brag enough about themselves like what we see in other geographies around the globe. The middle-America entrepreneurial movement is energized. There are real and clear advantages to building companies outside the traditional entrepreneurial hotspots. Here are three reasons why the heartland is hot when it comes to starting or scaling a business and why places like The NIIC attract global attention and have a world-class reputation:

1. **Smart right-fit talent.** The Midwest is home to Tier 1 research universities with strong commercialization centers, which, in turn, develop talented engineers, scientists, technologists, finance professionals. and even entrepreneurs. And they are staying here. Organizations like the Questa Education Foundation locally incentivize Indiana students to pursue work in the state following graduation and lessen their school debt making it more likely they can be entrepreneurial. A little-known fact is the amount of credit card debt a graduating college student has and the amount of school debt have caused millennials to have the lowest new venture formation rate of any age group. Our workforce tends to be scrappy and motivated. Our work ethic is unrivaled.

2. **Collaborative spirit.** Due in part to the how leaders and people do business in the Midwest, the level of access you have to other entrepreneurs, larger supply chain companies, and political leaders is remarkable. Also, there tends to be a mentality of paying it forward that has helped businesses of all sizes grow and thrive. Business leaders tend to be less guarded here when it comes to sharing knowledge and experience—and that's a boon for the entrepreneurial community. Finding and engaging mentors, trusted advisors, and people invested your success is a hallmark of the Midwest's reputation.

3. **Affordability but, more importantly, proximity.** Not everyone can afford to live in San Francisco. The Midwest is an attractive alternative to high-priced apartments, hourlong commutes, and the general stressors that come with big-city life. Fort Wayne in particular gets high marks for housing affordability. Home ownership for a middle-class family is in reach here, in contrast to coastal areas. Plus, from a business standpoint,

costs like real estate and taxes tend to be lower in the Midwest. Indiana is known to have a probusiness climate. There's a reason Salesforce was attracted to Indianapolis. It leased about 250,000 square feet in Indianapolis' tallest building and plans to expand its workforce significantly. In addition, Indiana is at the crossroads of the United States. You are able to get to nearly 90 percent of the US population in a day's drive, making us a magnet for the transportation and logistics industry. Amazon and many other companies have found this out.

Thought pause: *If you have relocated a business here from a bigger city outside the Midwest, what points of difference have you experienced here? If you have always been located in the Midwest, what are you doing to be known as a "best place to work"?*

On Creativity

We all need a certain amount of structure to get things done at work. But like anything, there's such thing as too much self-discipline. Carving out space in your schedule and enabling creativity to flourish in your physical space (think about where you do your best thinking) is important to the creative process. For example, Bill Gates carves out time by structuring learning around Think Weeks.

You might consider these tips to help carve out space for creativity in your business:

- **First things first.** Before you can go out there and consistently wow them with your next big idea, you have to ensure an appropriate balance in your wheel of life (physical, intellectual, emotional/relationships, and spiritual). Appropriate balancing of the four major factors is key to happiness. (Note, I did not say the four factors are equal in importance or in weight at a particular time in your life.)

- **Change your virtual habits.** The media you consume—whether for business or pleasure—matters and can affect your output. Read blogs and watch videos that inspire and motivate you to be better. TED.com is a prime example of such intellectual fodder. Also, tune in regularly to your mood. If you find that some content produces negative feelings, then consider taking a break from this type of material and find something that serves you. Without much political editorializing, we all need a break from the media after each tumultuous election cycle.

- **Recharge your batteries. (Make room for free time.)** Are you always plugged in? You could be doing yourself a disservice in the creativity department. You're best served to block out chunks of time during the week for recharging your mind and body. It's exciting to discover that when you allow for time for play with no clear focus, you create room for new ideas and spontaneity. Some of the best business ideas are conceived in this space.

- **Dream a little (or maybe a lot).** Over analysis is the kiss of death for innovation. Instead of picking apart every new idea that comes to mind, allow yourself the mental space to scheme and dream. You never know what next big idea could come out of some dream storming.

Thought pause: *Habits take focus, practice, and discipline. What one habit can you adopt this week to foster more creativity in your business and in your life?*

On Performance

There is no doubt that business owners face a lot of issues. I would be remiss not to mention imperatives pertaining to *starting* a new business. Here are three very practical things you need to consider before you make the leap (with the goal of reducing the performance dip—both the number and time in the dip) caused by problems, obstacles, crashes, and difficulties you might encounter during the start-up phase of your business.

- **Do you have the entrepreneurial talent?** This one may sound obvious, but plenty of well-intentioned people go into business without having thought this issue through clearly. The ability to sell is a talent that easily comes to mind. Sales (defined as ABC: always be closing) is the lifeblood of any venture. Regardless of the industry, the outlook does not look promising if the owner/founder lacks the ability or willingness to do the day-to-day work of the business. If you haven't taken the Gallup's Business Builder BP-10 assessment on-line, you should.

- **Know when to call in the experts.** If you are going to start a company, you must not only have passion for the difference your product/service/solution will make in the world, but you'll need to have business savvy and perseverance to work through the tough times or, at the very least, a team of people you can call on to take care of necessary management functions.

- **Know that with growth comes the need to let go.** You must remember that if your business is successful, it will grow. Growth is a mindset, and that's a good thing! There will come a time when you'll need to delegate doing the primary work of the business to others, stop growing, or hire someone to run the company while you continue to handle the primary work of the business. Before you embark, know which path you'll take. Be prepared for transitions and inflection points. Set benchmarks or triggers for critical decision-making activities.

Thought pause: *Make sure you have invested time to think about these three practical imperatives, and you'll thank yourself later. If you have recently started a business, what were the biggest challenges you faced in terms of human capital?*

On Burnout

Entrepreneurial burnout is more rampant than you might think. At best, people feel unmotivated on the job. At worst, they get to the point where they dread their work and can't stand the thought of another day. This doesn't make for a great entrepreneurial experience.

The key is to watch for telltale signs of burnout and tackle them head on. Consider these five important warning signs:

1. **That spark is gone.** No one is excited about work *every* day. Running a business can be thankless and unglamorous. There are always going to be trials and setbacks. If, however, you find yourself consistently unenthusiastic about going to work, then maybe you need to reassess your passion and revisit the choices you have made. Be sure to seek others out and be intentional in making changes in your life to achieve better work-life professional and personal satisfaction.

2. **You're easily irritated.** You're never going to get along with everybody all the time. But if you find yourself lashing out at coworkers, customers, or loved ones, you could be taking out your frustrations on them—instead of addressing the root of the problem. Be sure to be self-aware (brutally honest with yourself), intentional, and reflective.

3. **You're physically or mentally depleted.** Many entrepreneurs will regularly push themselves to the brink of exhaustion for the sake of success or self-preservation. But there is such a thing as too much. Mental anguish can manifest itself in the form of headaches, back pain, and other ailments.

   A little self-care can go a long way. Take time to eat well, exercise regularly, and get adequate sleep. Do yoga, get a massage, or listen to motivational speakers. Focus on the important things. Remember, it is not about time management but managing your energy. Be sure to distinguish results from activity. You don't want to be a hamster on a treadmill.

4. **You're having doubts.** Maybe you feel like you've put in a great deal of effort for little return. Or you might even question whether you should still be in business in the first place. This is the time to take a step back and do some honest, objective evaluation.

Seek out your coach or mentor for a third-party perspective so you don't let your bias cloud your judgment. Be sure to celebrate your small wins along the way!

5. **You feel detached or ineffectual.** You may be going through the motions, but you feel alienated or detached. When these thoughts come to mind, I find it's best to think back to the motivations that led you to start the business in the first place. Try to keep them front and center in your daily routine. Be sure to know your why. Simon Sinek reminds us that we need to know the purpose, cause, or belief that inspires us to do what we do. *What is your why?*

Thought pause: *Realize that you are only human, and burnout is an unfortunate tendency for entrepreneurial types. Don't look at it as a sign of failure but as a sign of passion. Just know when you need to reel yourself back in and take the steps to revive, renew, and reinvigorate your spirit. What tools or techniques do you employ to fight burnout?*

On Wellness

A study cited in *Inc.* magazine by Dr. Michael Freeman at the University of California San Francisco found that *49 percent of those who start a company say they have struggled with some form of mental illness in the past.* "Wellness is not just a buzz word du jour but an essential component of a healthier lifestyle for entrepreneurs and their families."

Sir Richard Branson opined in one of his blogs, "Mindfulness is one way that many entrepreneurs choose to combat the toll wrought by round-the-clock emails, long working hours and other aspects of our accelerated business culture."

But what is mindfulness? *Psychology Today* says, "Mindfulness is a state of active, open attention on the present. It means living in the moment and awakening to your current experience, rather than dwelling on the past or anticipating the future." The truth is, though, if you want to be at your best, you have to be willing to put in the time and effort. That means taking important steps to building and maintaining balance alongside working on your business.

Here are some of the basics to building healthier habits:

- **Carve out time for consistent exercise.** Rhythm is really important. Rhythm is about consistency so frequency matters more than time duration in the activity. Don't set yourself up for failure by overcommitting. Instead, ease into it. I need work in this area. Maybe start with a few days a week (walking, jogging, or cycling) and go from there. What's most important is that you find something you like. Engage an accountability buddy if you're worried about follow-through.

- **Plan your meals.** Food is fuel. Are you putting junk into your body? Your productivity will suffer over time. A steady diet of sugary, fatty, and greasy food will only make you crave more of it, thus putting you in a cycle of weight gain and lethargy. And that's no fun! Planning your meals is an easy way to stay on track, cut down on portion sizes, and eliminate or reducing some of the ingredients. I am known for asking for a third of the dressing on my salad. Even better would be not having salad dressing at all, but I can't do that yet. Also, cut down on those impulse decisions and stock healthier snacks - fruits and nuts.

- **Unplug and reset.** Our minds weren't meant for constant stimulation and noise. Take some time to unplug from technology and get outside. Don't forget about the importance of face-to-face interaction. No screen can ever replace that! Make it a point to schedule regular interactions (surround yourself with people who make you better) and participate in other activities that give you a release, such as yoga or meditation.

- **Sleep quality is number one.** Try to maintain a consistent sleep schedule by going to sleep and getting up at the same time every day. Avoid working and eating in your bed. If you work in your bed, your mind might associate it with stress, which can affect the quality of your sleep. It's proven that when we're well rested, we have sharper minds and healthier bodies. Sleep deficiencies can lead to chronic diseases and increased health risks. Sleep Cycle is a great app for measuring your sleep quality and activity levels.

- **Use technology.** Apps like MyFitnessPal, iHealth, Health, or others can help you track your activity, diet, exercise, and plug into a community of support. Many are free but have additional opt-in, fee-based features that can help you stay on track.

Thought pause: *Which of the five wellness tips is most difficult for you? What tips or tricks have you found to be effective in staying healthy in terms of mind, body, and soul?*

People and Talent

Insights Dashboard

Topic	Thought Pause	Insights/Field Work
On the Midwest Advantage	If you have relocated a business here from a bigger city outside the Midwest, what points of difference have you experienced here? If you have always been located in the Midwest, what are you doing to be known as a "best place to work"?	What is your community's secret sauce? What does your community do better than anyone else? (Bragging Rights?); and What differentiates your community and makes it special?
On Creativity	Habits take focus, practice, and discipline. What one habit can you adopt this week to foster more creativity in your business and in your life?	Where do you get your best ideas? Who brings out the best ideas in you? How is your personal self-awareness? What do you want to work on, develop, and mature in to be a better version of yourself?

Topic	Thought Pause	Insights/Field Work
On Performance	Make sure you have put the time in to think about these three practical imperatives, and you'll thank yourself later. If you have recently started a business, what were the biggest challenges you faced in terms of human capital?	Have you asked someone who knows you well, works with you, or is your boss: What am I doing that you really like? What should I stop doing? And do you think I am adding value to the organization? Take control of your career. You are in charge.
On Burnout	Realize that you are only human, and burnout is an unfortunate tendency for entrepreneurial types. Don't look at it as a sign of failure but as a sign of passion. Just know when you need to reel yourself back in and take the steps to revive, renew, and reinvigorate your spirit. What tools or techniques do you employ to fight burnout? Which of the five wellness tips is most difficult for you? What tips or tricks have you found to be effective in staying healthy in terms of mind, body, and soul?	Work-life balance. How do you measure it? How are you doing today on a scale of 1–5 (5 being perfect)? Where do you want to be on the scale in 12 months? Consider the powerful questions identified in Matthew Kelly's book **Off Balance** (https://www.floydconsulting.com/resources).

Author Biography

Karl R. LaPan is a business professional with more than thirty years of experience in consumer, industrial, technology, health care services, and financial companies. Since 2000, he has served as president and CEO of the Northeast Indiana Innovation Center/Park (The NIIC), a high-tech, high-touch fifty-five-acre entrepreneurial community dedicated to accelerating the growth of innovative companies.

LaPan is a student of business and entrepreneurship. He is an in-demand thought leader and speaker on customer service, loyalty, creativity and innovation, marketing and management strategy, entrepreneurial growth, business and strategic planning, and leadership. He has been the recipient of several local and regional awards and has authored and coauthored numerous books, articles, and blogs on business innovation, creativity, and entrepreneurship.

As an educator, LaPan was previously an associate faculty member in the MBA program at Indiana University – Purdue University Fort Wayne (School of Business and Management Sciences) and served as an adjunct professor of Marketing and Executive in Residence at Taylor University's MBA program.

In his community leadership role, LaPan serves on advisory boards at Science Central, a hands-on science and technology children's museum. He is also an advisory board member of the University of Florida Sid Martin Biotechnology Center. In addition, his board service extends to several local innovative start-up companies (BioPoly LLC and Allied Payment Network) and well-established regional health care and financial services companies (PHP of Northern Indiana and iAB Financial Bank until its recent sale). He was also a visiting professor at the University of International Business and Economics (UIBE) 2016 Summer School (Beijing, China) where he taught a course on entrepreneurship titled Entrepreneurial Pathways. He is also the former board chair of the International Business Innovation Association (InBIA).

Lifelong learning is a priority for LaPan. He holds a BS (high honors, Summa Cum Laude) in Business Management from Franklin Pierce University and a MS in Human Resource Development from the American University in Washington, DC. He is a graduate of the prestigious General Electric's Financial Management Program and has completed all five of the professional development programs offered by the Disney Institute. In 2013, he completed the

Harvard University Strategic Perspectives in Nonprofit Management Program. Prior to Harvard, he completed Stanford University's Executive Program for Non-Profit Leaders in 2010. Recently, he completed the Certified Innovation Mentor Program (CIMP) at the University of Notre Dame. LaPan also holds an Indiana real estate broker license and numerous professional certifications.

Outside of his professional life, his main interests and pursuits are innovation in education, health care, and technology. He is married to Kelly, and together, they have three sons, Griffin, Drake, and Brayden.

www.TheNiic.Org

Dream Big. Get Real.

Bonus: All Good Things Come in 3's

On Side Hustles

The gig economy is alive and growing. Nearly forty percent of Americans report having a "side hustle," which could range in focus from fixing computers, moonlighting as a consultant or programmer to driving for Uber. Many of these "hustlers" are Millennials, but more and more older workers are turning to contingent worker status as well. *So, what can a side gig teach a potential entrepreneur or business builder?* Turns out, a side hustle may be ground school for entrepreneurship if the motivation is opportunity-based and not necessity-based. Here's why:

1) **Side jobs require discipline.** Entrepreneurs need to manage time properly because they know every hour away from their business is potentially lost time. Gen Y'ers who work side gigs are also used to having to work hard and long hours to achieve their goals. This means it's not as rude of awakening if they decide to go it alone full time. Successful hustlers have already have shown they have the motivation and stick-to-it-ness necessary to have a fighting chance in the marketplace. (Remember, Angela Duckworth's definition of grit is passion + perseverance. In my mind, stick-to-it-ness is "dogged" perseverance.)

2) **It can be a way to bootstrap an enterprise.** Starting a business costs money. And with crippling student loan debt, many Gen Y'ers do not have the funds to invest in a full-fledged operation, from the outset. This is why side jobs hold so much potential--this secondary income can be put towards startup costs to lessen that burden and properly capitalize your new company or venture.

3) **There's less pressure.** Walking away from a stable, full-time job to pursue a venture might be perceived by family or friends as risky. This puts a great deal of stress on the person. The business needs to cover its operating costs, invest in its capabilities and do more than just provide income replacement for the owners There can be many sleepless nights, wondering if you're going to weather the ups and downs of a new startup. However, with a side gig, the investment tends to be minimal, and therefore the opportunity cost is less. It's easier to walk away from a floundering side gig. However, if the side gig is well received, they might be able to turn a side hustle into a full-time enterprise.

Thought pause: *Many successful enterprises started as a side gig. Do you have a side hustle you'd like to take to the next level? Have you realistically assessed your commitment, time management and energy level to ensure you can handle the additional work burden?*